DEBORAH KNEEN'S
AUSTRALIAN WILDFLOWER SAMPLER

Also by Deborah Kneen:

The Australian Folk Art Collection

DEBORAH KNEEN'S
AUSTRALIAN WILDFLOWER SAMPLER

DESIGNS FOR DECORATIVE PAINTING

Copyright © 1990 by Deborah Kneen

ISBN 0 646 01608 3

All Rights Reserved. No part of this book may be reproduced by photocopying or any other form of mechanical or electronic reproduction *except* to reduce or enlarge patterns for personal use only.

Disclaimer
The information in this instruction book is presented in good faith. However, no warranty is given, nor results guaranteed, nor is freedom from any patent to be inferred. Since we have no control over the physical conditions surrounding the application of the information contained in this book, the publisher and the author disclaim any liability for untoward results.

Published by Tracy Marsh Publications Pty. Ltd.
94 Wright Street, Adelaide, South Australia.

First published 1990

Printed at Stock Journal Printing Pty. Ltd.,
24 Hindmarsh Avenue, Welland, South Australia.

*So live that only the most
beautiful wildflowers
Will spring up where you
have dwelt*

Thoreau

ACKNOWLEDGMENTS

I am indebted to many people whose encouragement, generosity, assistance and technical advice have helped me to create this book.

Special thanks to Elizabeth Adair, Judy Allen, June Bibby, Robert and Virginia Brown, June and Syd Cooper, Betty Downy, Pamela Firth, Joanne and Mark Hill, Else Jeppesen, Lisa Johnson, Pamela Jones, Denis McDermott, Tracy Marsh and the staff at Tracy Marsh Publications Pty Ltd., Joy Milne, Christine Moss, Jan Norris, Harvey Shields, Joyce Spencer and the Sutherland painting group, Pauline Tomkinson, Dora Wilson and all the friends and colleagues with whom I've had the pleasure to paint over the past years.

Particular thanks to Richard Dawes-Cross who kindly allowed me to quote from the beautiful book, 'Australian Bushland Fairies' (Anvil Press), by his late wife, Isabel Dawes.

And, as always, a very big thank you to my Mum, Phyll, husband, Peter, and little son, Brenton. Without their love, support, practical help and advice, this book would not have been possible.

PREFACE

*'To see a World in a grain of sand,
And a Heaven in a wild flower.'*
William Blake

Wildflowers have always provided inspiration for the craft enthusiast. And if you love the beautiful wildflowers that grow in the Australian countryside, you will also love them growing under your paintbrush!

This sampler presents a variety of Australian wildflower designs to be adapted to the decorative painting projects of your choice. The designs can be applied to any number of surfaces: wood, metal, canvas, paper, fabric, glass, leather, unglazed porcelain, terracotta ... the possibilities are virtually unlimited.

Using Australian wildflowers, you can create unique hand-painted collectables, gifts, furniture, garments, and jewellery. And it's fun to produce artwork which can actually be *used*, not simply hung on the wall.

Have confidence in your innate artistic talent. Decorative painting has opened up a new world for many people *who were always artistic but just didn't know it.*

A decorative painter need not conform to the rules of formal art. Your painted flowers do not have to look realistic because the aim is an impressionistic rather than an exact botanical representation. The degree to which you simplify and stylise the flowers is up to you. But if your work is pleasing to the eye, and executed on a properly prepared and finished surface; then you have achieved the most important goals of decorative painting.

Whether you choose to paint Australian wildflowers on a T-shirt, a bangle, a plate, a piece of furniture, or indeed any of the hundreds of other possible projects, I hope that you will enjoy your decorative painting experiences. And if you do, your enjoyment will be reflected in your work.

Happy painting!

Deborah

Dedicated in loving memory
to my father, Raymond
Arthur Hill 1927-1990

CONTENTS

PREFACE

**INTRODUCTION: WILDFLOWERS AND AUSTRALIAN
DECORATIVE PAINTING**   11

CHAPTER 1: THE BASICS   13
  Safety First   14
  Surface Preparation, Decorating Procedures, and Finishing   15
    Wood   15
    Metal   18
    Fabric   19
    Canvas   20
    Straw   21
    Papier Mâché   21
    Bisque Porcelain   22
    Candles   22
    Terracotta   23
    Glass   23
    Leather   24
    Paper   24

CHAPTER 2: DESIGN TIPS   33
  Enlarging and Reducing Patterns   34
  Transferring Patterns   34
  Creating Your Own Designs   35
    Design Principles   36
    Symmetrical and Asymmetrical Designs   37
    Adding Interest   37
    The Design Process   38
    Designing Borders   39

CHAPTER 3: DESIGNING WITH AUSTRALIAN WILDFLOWERS   49
  Using Australian Wildflowers in Place of European Motifs   50
  A Basic Drawing and Painting Guide to Forty Australian Wildflowers   53
  Facts About the Wildflowers   70

CHAPTER 4: WILDFLOWER PATTERNS   73
  Posies, Sprays, Baskets, and Garlands   74
  Festive and Special Occasion Designs   91
  Borders   97

APPENDIX   103
  Lettering and Numerals   104
  Useful Addresses   107
  Further Reading   108

INDEX   109

COLOUR WORKSHEETS

	Page
State Floral Emblems	25, 26, 27, 28
Large Wildflowers	29, 30
Native Daisies	31
Christmas Wildflowers	32, 41, 42
Small and Filler Flowers	43, 44, 45
Borders	46, 47
Wildflower Sprays	48, 81
Native Passion Flower Trellis	82
Homestead Wreath	83
Waratah Babies	84
Rosella Bride	85
Wildflower Advent Calender	86, 87
Wildflower Alphabet	88

INTRODUCTION:
WILDFLOWERS AND AUSTRALIAN DECORATIVE PAINTING

If you are used to painting roses, daisies, and tulips in your folk art designs, why not try substituting waratahs, flannel flowers, or any of the wealth of native Australian flora? After all, there is a definite historical tradition for the use of Australian wildflower motifs in our decorative arts.

In folk painting, however, Australia has never had the strong tradition of Europe and North America.

In the eighteenth and nineteenth centuries European and American farmers and settlers used the long, cold winters when they were confined indoors to pursue many popular crafts, as their museums of folk art now testify.

Australia's early colonial settlers led difficult lives with little leisure time. They faced a particularly harsh landscape and climate and the constant threat of drought, bushfire or flood. There was little time to indulge in crafts of any kind.

For most of the nineteenth century, folk and decorative painting was virtually unknown in Australia. But there were notable exceptions. German settlers in places like the Barossa Valley of South Australia continued to paint the traditional Bauernmalerei designs which they had brought from their homeland. They used motifs such as roses, hearts, and scrolls to decorate chairs, trunks, wardrobes, and cradles.

Towards the end of the nineteenth century, crafts in general began to enjoy a popularity never before seen in Australia. This interest stemmed from a number of factors, both local and imported.

The Arts and Crafts Movement

The influence of the English Arts and Crafts Movement, led by William Morris, was making itself felt in Australia. Morris was a political activist, poet, and prolific designer of furniture, textiles, and wallpaper. His movement was a reaction against the industrialised and urbanised society of nineteenth-century England with its proliferating factories and crowded, dirty cities.

Morris felt that the growth of mass production had debased the applied arts and degraded the craftsman. He believed that articles produced by hand are aesthetically and morally superior to machine-made work because they allow the craftsperson to make his or her own creative contribution. His influence was so far-reaching that his designs are still being used today.

The Influence of Federation

In the last two decades of the nineteenth century the Australian colonies were moving towards Federation. One aspect of this movement was a strong growth in nationalism which soon created a fervour for Australian motifs in architecture and the decorative arts.

Painted wildflowers were widely used in domestic interiors and public buildings. Wildflower friezes were stencilled at dado, picture-rail and cornice level on walls; the waratah and flannel flower being particular favourites in stencil designs. Native flower motifs were also hand-painted on stained-glass windows, glass door panels and fanlights.

Waratah stencil design, 1906

Huon pine table with wreath of Tasmanian wildflowers, painted by Miss H. Bell, Hobart, c. 1880.

Genteel Accomplishments

At the same time Australia was experiencing an economic boom and the emergence of a prosperous middle class with the wealth, leisure time, and inclination to pursue 'genteel accomplishments'.

The decorative arts collection of the National Gallery in Canberra includes late nineteenth-century hand-painted furniture and household accessories decorated by amateur painters, often the ladies of the newly prosperous households. They sought to make beautifully crafted pieces to decorate their homes, just as we do today. Their decorative painting work included boxes, screens, chests of drawers and table-tops which they painted with garlands and wreaths of native flowers or with fernwork designs known as 'spatterwork'.

The twentieth century brought an increase in machine-made furniture and utensils and a trend away from decoration and embellishment. With the arrival of mass production, hand-painted items fell out of favour.

Spatterwork chest of drawers Tas. c. 1890

Current Trends

The revival in the 1970s and 1980s of traditional arts and crafts mirrors that of the late nineteenth century. Today's craftspeople and hobbyists are affirming the old-fashioned values of hearth and home and celebrating the beauty of pieces crafted and decorated by hand. Folk and decorative painting, in particular, is growing in popularity. Painting groups and shops are springing up all over the country as people realise that *these art forms are accessible to everyone*, not just professional artisans and those with formal training or so-called 'artistic ability'.

By using Australian wildflowers in our projects, we are continuing a nineteenth-century tradition and at the same time consolidating a truly Australian style of folk and decorative art.

Painted desert pea on ceramic tile, 1905

> *'They will maintain the state of the world,
> And all their desire is in the work of their craft.'*
> Ecclesiasticus 38:34

If you would like to become involved in the world of folk and decorative painting, refer to the Appendix for a list of folk art businesses that will supply information on materials and classes.

Close-up of the table-top in the collection of the Australian National Gallery.

Gum blossoms painted on a tile, 1905

CHAPTER 1
THE BASICS

SAFETY FIRST

• When sanding wood, especially medium-density fibreboard, take the piece outside and wear a disposable surgical mask, available from pharmacies. Wear a plastic apron to shield your clothing from dust.

• Whenever possible, use products labelled 'non toxic'. Some American products are labelled 'A P Non Toxic', which indicates they have been subjected to fairly rigorous toxicological testing. There is no such standard as yet for Australian-made art products. Most of the preparation, painting, and finishing instructions in this book are based on non-toxic products. If you are unsure about the toxicity of a product, check the label. If it carries the words 'use in a well-ventilated space' or 'clean up with turps', you can be reasonably certain there are some nasty chemicals involved.

• Water-based acrylic paints are 'non toxic', but remember that paints were not meant to be swallowed or inhaled! So don't put a paintbrush in your mouth to clean or groom it. And wash pigments off your hands, particularly before preparing food. Take care with cadmium colours and try to substitute a different red, orange, or yellow.

• Try to avoid aerosols—for instance, aerosol paint or varnish. You can achieve the same or better effects with a brush. And it's far more economical. After all, artists managed very well for centuries before the invention of aerosols.

• If you have to use oil-based products, consider wearing a mask and applying a barrier cream to your hands or wearing protective gloves. Always use odourless turpentine. Do not work on your projects or clean up your painting materials in food preparation areas.

• You should only need to use oil-based products for procedures such as metal preparation and specialised varnishing. Water-based products will do almost all the jobs formerly assigned to oil-based and petroleum-based products.

• Dispose of leftover paint from your palette by wrapping it and putting it in the bin, not down the sink. Pour dirty painting water and mediums over the weeds in your garden, not into the drains. Some painters even swear by dirty painting water as a fertiliser for their plants!

SURFACE PREPARATION, DECORATING PROCEDURES, AND FINISHING

We are sometimes so keen to paint our designs that we neglect the most important steps: *thorough preparation and protective finishing*. By following the correct preparation and finishing techniques, you will ensure that your work looks beautiful for many years.

The following section on Wood describes decorating procedures that are applicable to all surfaces. Since the emphasis of this book is on design rather than on painting technique there is only a brief discussion of decorating procedures. My book *The Australian Folk Art Collection* contains detailed information on materials, brushstrokes, and painting technique.

WOOD
PREPARATION
Old Wood
If an old wood piece is painted with a sound coverage of paint there is no need to strip the paint. Simply rub it down with sandpaper (see 'Sanding', page 15) to give a good ground for the new paint. If the original paint is gloss, it is particularly important to remove the shine or the new paint will not adhere.

Stripping
Old paint that is cracking, flaking, or blistering must be removed to give a smooth surface. You will also need to remove old varnish. First clean off dirt with a damp cloth and a little detergent.

Paint and varnish can be softened with proprietary paint stripper. Make sure to work outside and to wear protective gloves and a disposable face mask. Remove any metal hardware, such as hinges or handles, before stripping.

Allow the stripper to soften the old paint, causing it to blister. Then scrape off as much as you can, completing the job with coarse sandpaper or steel wool. To remove thick paint, you will need to repeat applications of paint stripper.

After using paint stripper, wipe over the surface with a solution of white vinegar to prevent any remaining traces of stripper from attacking the subsequent painted finish from beneath.

Filling
Fill any holes or cracks with proprietary wood filler. Always allow the filler to dry thoroughly. Then rub with medium sandpaper in the direction of the grain until the surface is smooth. If there are any large holes, you may have to fill them with plastic wood.

Sanding
To ensure even sanding pressure, make a sanding block by tearing off a neat rectangle of sandpaper and wrapping it around a block of wood. You can use this sanding block for flat surfaces. When sanding a curved surface, fold the sandpaper in half and hold it in your fingers.

If the surface itself or crosscuts on the end grain are very rough, begin with a coarse sandpaper to wear away the uneven surface quickly. Work your way through a medium paper down to a fine one or fine steel wool for final sanding. Always work in the direction of the grain, rubbing backwards and forwards, not in circles. Sand carefully near edges and carved details.

Wipe the surface clean with a dry tack cloth (a damp cloth could raise the grain of the wood). Check corners and crevices for sanding dust.

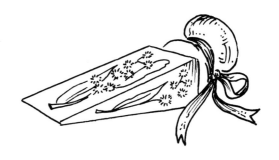

New Wood

Follow the instructions for filling and sanding, under 'Old Wood'.

Sealing

Sealing is used to give 'tooth' and grip to a surface, to create a strong bond between the surface and the paint. It also prevents tannin stains from seeping through. Sealing is not necessary if you plan to stain (page 16) or pickle (page 16), as these background techniques can be done on raw wood.

Otherwise, whether you seal or not depends on the type of wood, the effect you want to achieve, and your own personal preference. Some people seal everything; others rarely seal anything. It is worth noting that modern acrylic paints contain polymers that act as sealers. I think it is advisable to seal medium-density fibreboard, which tends to be very porous, and also any timber with heavy knots.

When sealing, you can take a short cut by sealing and base-coating in the one step. Mix approximately equal parts all-purpose sealer (or water-based satin varnish) and the acrylic paint colour of your choice, and use this for the first base coat.

Base-Coating

If you want opaque paint coverage, base-coat the piece in the colour of your choice. Use artists' acrylic paints for an heirloom piece. Some people economise and use acrylic house paint to base-coat large items—the long-term quality is inferior, but the choice is yours. Use a large synthetic brush or a sponge brush and aim for a smooth finish. Two or even three coats may be necessary, depending on the transparency of the paint colour. Allow each coat to dry thoroughly before applying the next, and rub down between coats with a brown-paper bag to smooth the surface.

Acrylic Staining

Acrylic staining is suitable for a wood item with an attractive grain. (If the surface is heavily knotted or has been filled, it may be preferable to use an opaque base coat instead). You do not need to seal the item before acrylic staining, because the sealer-varnish in the acrylic staining mixture is sufficient to seal the surface.

Mix approximately five parts all-purpose sealer (or clear glazing medium or water-based satin-finish varnish) with one part paint. It is better for the staining mixture to be too thin than too heavy. You can always give the item a second or third application of stain, but you cannot easily remove a coat that is too heavy.

Work with a large brush or cloth that is wet, but not dripping with stain. Apply the stain quickly in the direction of the grain and only over an area that you can conveniently handle. Use long smooth strokes. Wipe off with a soft cloth, again using long strokes in the direction of the grain. This will even the colour and take out any lines or marks previously made. You need to work quickly because, if the stain dries in each section, edge marks and overlapping will appear. Keep the edge 'alive'. Do not allow it to dry out before you have covered the next portion of the surface. If the edge does dry out, it will be less noticeable because you are working *with the grain* rather than across it.

End grains are very open and will soak up extra stain, so they tend to stain darker than the rest of the wood. You can prevent this by mixing a small amount of very weak stain (say, ten parts sealer-varnish to one part paint) and applying it to the end grain. If the effect is too light, you can apply extra stain until the tone matches that of the rest of the work. Raised details and carving will also need a weaker mixture.

Some suggested paint colours to mix with the sealer-varnish to make a stain are:

- raw sienna
- burnt sienna
- burnt umber
- brown earth
- or any combinations of the above

If possible, test the stain on a sample piece of wood or begin staining in an unobtrusive place, such as the back or bottom of the item. Before decorating, rub the stained surface with a paper bag.

Pickling

Pickling is a pale, whitewashed effect used for furniture and household accessories. It was originally used as a cost-saving finish to make paint go further. Mix a small amount of pastel acrylic paint (cream, opal, ash pink, etc.) with all-purpose sealer or water-based satin-finish varnish. Paint the mixture on with a large brush. Work quickly and methodically, covering one section at a time. The application technique is similar to that of staining. Rub off any excess with a soft cloth, again working with the grain. If the effect is too pale, repeat the process. Marks and overlapping edges will be less noticeable than with staining because the pickling colour is so pale. When dry, rub with a brown-paper bag.

DECORATING PROCEDURES

The ideal paints for decorating a wooden item are artists' acrylics, available in tubes, bottles, and jars. Students' acrylics are not of the same quality and will not give the flow or coverage needed. You could also experiment with permanent marking pens and permanent ink, particularly for liner work. I have even used fabric puff paint and dimensional markers with success on wood. Be adventurous!

Below is a brief outline of the basic decorative painting procedures that are applicable to *all* surfaces.

1. Block in the main areas of colour in your design by base-painting them in colouring-book fashion (in other words, stay within the lines and paint a smooth, solid area of colour). You may need several coats for good coverage. For this blocking in or base-painting, you generally use a medium value of the appropriate colour. For example, in painting wattle, you would base-coat the balls in medium yellow.

2. For shadows, shade with a darker value of the base colour. In the wattle example, you could shade the balls with a touch of raw sienna.

3. The areas that receive more light will need to be highlighted with a light value of the base colour. For wattle, try pale yellow, cream, or white.

4. Using a fine liner brush, add outlines or fine detailing. Remember to mix water or an appropriate medium with the paint to give good flow. The paint should be the consistency of Indian ink. For the wattle example, you would now use a fine brush to paint the tiny furry lines around the edge of each ball.

FINISHING

First make sure that the paint is thoroughly dry and that the surface is free of dust, lint, brush hairs, and so on. I recommend using a *water-based* satin or gloss finish varnish such as Delta Ceramcoat (see 'Safety First' on page 14). It dries quickly and so you can apply many coats in the one day.

Remember that numerous thin coats are better than a few thick coats. The number of coats required will depend on the intended use of the item. Four to six coats should be sufficient for decorative pieces, whereas up to twelve coats will be needed for an item that will be exposed to heavy use.

If the item is likely to be exposed to water and alcohol stains or to heat (for instance, trays, coasters, placemats), use a *polyurethane* water-based satin or gloss varnish such as Jo Sonja's satin or Derivan Matisse satin or gloss. Four to six coats are required and the piece will not reach maximum durability until the varnish is cured—about two to four weeks. During that time take care to avoid exposing the item to heat and moisture.

For a truly professional finish, rub down the last few coats of varnish. Do not rub down until you have first applied two or three initial coats of varnish; otherwise you could cut through the thin layer of varnish and damage the painted surface beneath. Make sure that the varnish is dry; then, using fine sandpaper or fine steel wool, rub lightly in the one direction, not in circles. If the wood grain is evident, rub in the direction of the grain.

Note: Rubbing down is particularly important when using gloss varnish.

You should *not* rub the final coat of varnish down with sandpaper or steel wool. Substitute a brown-paper bag or nylon pantihose. As a final step (and this is very much a matter of personal taste), you may wish to paste-wax the surface and then buff with a soft cloth to give a rich sheen.

Basic Decorating Procedures

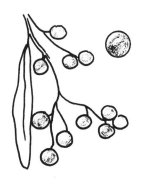
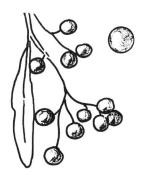
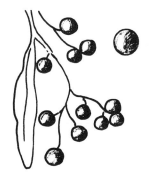
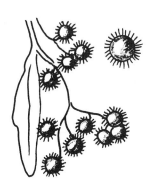

Base-coat
Diagram 1

Highlight
Diagram 2

Shade
Diagram 3

Details
Diagram 4

METAL

PREPARATION

Metal always needs more preparation than wood because of its susceptibility to chipping and rust.

New, Unprimed Metal

New, unprimed metal has an oily film to protect it from rust. But if you intend to paint the metal, you must remove this film because the paint cannot adhere to it. Remove the film with a solution of approximately half water and half vinegar. Dry the item well with a hair dryer on a low setting, making sure that all seams and corners are dry. Remember that any trapped moisture will cause rust in the future. If the metal is shiny, sand in the one direction with fine steel wool or sandpaper in order to give some grip to the surface. Clean with a tack cloth.

Prime the metal with a proprietary rust-preventive primer, for example, Penetrol. Apply the primer smoothly as it tends to be thick and can develop ridges. Leave the primer to dry as the instructions direct, usually for 24 to 48 hours. Then rub smooth with a brown-paper bag as sandpaper may damage the surface.

Base-coat with the artists' acrylic colour of your choice.

Galvanised Metal

Galvanised metal has a coating of zinc to protect it from corrosion. First buff lightly with fine steel wool and wipe clean. Then apply one or two coats of galvanised iron primer. When dry, base-coat as usual.

Old Metal

If the surface is in bad condition, consider having it professionally prepared. Note that sandblasting or grit blasting is suitable for solid items but not for thin metal.

To remove dirt, wash in a solution of equal parts water and vinegar. Dry thoroughly. Remove heavy rust with a wire brush or steel wool. Then apply a proprietary rust remover such as those used for cars. Read the manufacturer's instructions carefully and work outside, wearing protective gloves and a disposable mask. You may need to repeat this rust-removal process several times.

Next apply a rust-preventive primer. Two or three coats should give long-term protection. Leave each coat to dry as the instructions direct (for a day or two), buffing between coats with a brown-paper bag.

Finally, base-coat as for new metal.

Primed, Rust-Free Metal

If the piece is already primed and rust-free, check for any scratches or chips and touch them up with primer. This is essential to prevent moisture from seeping in and causing rust.

All Metal

Hint: To harden the based-coated surface of small metal items prior to decorating, it is advisable to heat-treat the item by placing it in a low oven for half an hour. Never use a high temperature as this will weaken the solder. Turn the oven to the lowest setting until it is warm. Turn the oven off and put the item in, keeping the door slightly ajar.

Note: It is recommended that metal preparation should not be undertaken if the humidity level is above 85%. Similarly, if you leave a piece unvarnished (i.e. unsealed) for any length of time, particularly in wet weather, spots of rust may appear.

DECORATING PROCEDURES

The decorating procedures are the same as for wood (see page 15), but do not thin the paint too much with water or other mediums.

FINISHING

Make sure that the item is free of dust, brush hairs, and so on before varnishing. Metalware is more prone to scratches and chips than wood so it tends to need more coats of varnish. I would suggest a minimum of six coats of water-based varnish. Allow each coat to dry thoroughly before applying the next. Avoid using sandpaper as sanding may damage the surface, particularly on corners and edges. Try pantihose or a brown-paper bag instead. Finally, if you want a rich sheen, finish with a coat of paste wax and buff with a soft cloth.

Look after the decorative metal piece and do not clean it with strong chemicals or abrasives. A regular gentle wipe with a dusting cloth will keep it looking perfect.

FABRIC
PREPARATION
Choice of Fabric

Use smooth washable fabrics such as cotton, cotton blends, cotton and polyester, linen, denim, calico. Avoid heavily textured or nobbly fabrics because the paint will not adhere well to them. Knit fabrics are generally too stretchy to give successful results. And any fabric that has been treated with water repellent will not allow the paint to penetrate. Silk is a suitable surface for fabric painting but silk painting is an art form in itself and the techniques and materials required are beyond the scope of this book.

Background Colours

You do not have to choose a white or cream fabric. Decorative designs, particularly wildflowers, look attractive on coloured backgrounds too. But remember that your perception of a colour will be different when that colour is painted over a coloured background. For example, blue paint will look blue on a white background but will take on a greenish tone on a yellow background. On a dark background you may need to use extra coats of paint for good coverage.

Testing

It is advisable to test any fabric with which you are unfamiliar for its suitability as a surface for decorative painting. Take a sample, wash it, then paint a small area and allow it to dry. Heat-set (if appropriate to the particular paint used) and wash again. It is particularly important to test the durability of items that will be heavily used, such as placemats and tablecloths. After painting and heat-setting the sample, wash several times to check for fading or change in colour.

Preparing the Fabric

Wash the fabric before painting, following the directions on the label. Do not use fabric softener. The washing process will remove any sizing in the fabric. Sizing can interfere with the bonding process between the paint and the fabric. You can then iron the fabric to give a smooth surface for painting.

Setting Up A Work Area

It is vital to keep your work area and your hands clean if you are to avoid getting smudges on the fabric. When painting T-shirts, windcheaters, and so on, place a sheet of cardboard covered in plastic wrap inside the garment and under the area to be painted to prevent the paint from seeping through to the underside of the garment.

Making Your Own Garments

If you are making a garment yourself, it is usually easier to paint the design before assembling the garment. But remember to allow for seams and to sew darts before painting.

Placement of Design

When transferring a design to fabric, make as few marks as possible as they are often difficult to remove, even with 'water erasable' transfer pens. If you are an experienced painter, paint the design freehand. For the technicalities of transferring designs to fabric, see page 35.

If you want to place your design in the centre of a square piece of fabric, you can find the centre by folding the fabric in half, and then in half again. For a rectangular piece of fabric like a placemat, fold the fabric diagonally. In each case, the centre is where the two folds intersect. See diagrams 1 and 2.

Diagram 1

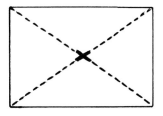

Diagram 2

DECORATING PROCEDURES

Fabric artists have the choice of using proprietary fabric paints or artists' acrylics mixed with textile medium (also known as 'fabric fixative'). Some of the proprietary fabric paints need to be heat-set, but many of the newer paints are permanent without heat-setting. Always read the manufacturer's instructions carefully. There is an exciting array of fabric paints on the market. They are available in jars, tubes, bottles, and even as paint pens. You will find paints that allow you to create fluorescent, pearlescent, crystallised, marbleised, metallic, three-dimensional, glittery and many more effects.

With dimensional paint pens you can make raised stamens and centre dots. You can outline stems and leaves in metallics and puff up petals and centres with puff paint.

Artists' Acrylics and Textile Medium

If you decide to adapt your artists' acrylics for fabric painting, you will need to add textile medium so that the paint can penetrate the fibre of the fabric. Mix approximately two parts paint with one part medium. You do not need to be exact about this mixture. When your painting is dry, it must be heat-set (although those of you who have accidentally smudged acrylic paint on a garment will probably argue that it is already permanent!)

Fabric Painting Tips

When you apply the paint to fabric, scrub it into the fibres, following the grain of the fabric. You will find this much easier and smoother than painting across the grain of the fabric which causes stretching.

Fabric paints, if applied thickly, take a long time to dry. To speed up drying time as you paint, use a hair dryer. To avoid smudges, paint from the top of the item to the bottom whenever possible. Wash your hands regularly to remove all paint. When working on a large item such as a tablecloth, use a little caution and you will avoid accidents. Paint one section at a time, allowing it to dry before moving to the next. Keep any areas not being painted out of harm's way by covering them with a clean cloth or a sheet of plastic. You may even be able to bundle excess fabric into a plastic bag.

If you do accidentally smudge your work, try to remove the stain immediately. Spot-clean with a damp cloth and mild soap. If that does not remove the spot, try nail polish remover or vodka (but not on silk or delicate fabrics).

If all else fails, try covering the spot by working in an extra design element such as a small filler flower or leaf.

Use of Thickener

Thickener is a useful product which helps to prevent the paint bleeding on fabrics like silk and polyester. It also assists in keeping the texture of the fabric supple in areas where fabric paint is applied. Before painting, scrub the thickener onto the areas covered by your design, using an old brush. Keep within the design outlines. The thickener should be wet when the paint is applied over it. If you are ready to paint a particular area and the thickener has dried, simply scrub on a second coat. The thickener evaporates on drying.

FINISHING

When the paint is thoroughly dry, heat-set it (where applicable) to make the design permanent. Place a clean white handkerchief or tea-towel between the fabric and the iron to protect the painted surface from direct heat. Set the iron on dry (not steam) and heat to the wool setting. Hold the iron on each section for 30 seconds to lock in the colours. For thick fabrics, repeat this process on the wrong side of the garment.

I recommend handwashing painted fabric items and drying them naturally, away from direct sunlight. (Electric clothes dryers can damage puff, glitter, and other special effects or cause 'pilling' on a windcheater).

CANVAS
PREPARATION

Canvas items such as tote bags, directors' chair covers, and window blinds need no preparation. Do not be tempted to pre-wash these items. Although you must wash other fabric articles to remove the sizing before painting, pre-washing canvas will make it limp.

DECORATING PROCEDURES

The decorating procedures for canvas are the same as for fabric (see page 19). But use proprietary fabric paints that do not require heat-setting.

Canvas items look best with simple designs. For window blinds a simple border treatment, perhaps echoing a wallpaper or curtain motif, is most suitable.

FINISHING

To protect against soiling, allow the paint to cure (about two weeks). Then spray the surface with Scotchgard. Use a damp cloth and mild soap to wipe off any marks. Note that exposure to sun and rain will fade and damage the design in time.

STRAW

Straw items suitable for decorating include hats and bags.

PREPARATION

Straw hats and bags need no special preparation, but the surface may be easier to paint if you apply one coat of all-purpose sealer before decorating.

DECORATING PROCEDURES

Paint the design directly onto the unpainted straw. There is no need to base-coat—the natural straw provides an attractive backdrop.

Note that the textured surface will make liner work and detailing difficult, so try to keep your designs simple. Straw items lend themselves to simple, stylised designs.

FINISHING

Finish with one or two coats of water-based satin varnish. This will protect the item and allow you to wipe the surface with a slightly damp cloth to remove any dust that may accumulate during storage.

PAPIER MÂCHÉ

Literally 'chewed paper', the French term papier mâché (pronounced 'par-pee-yay mar-shay') refers to shapes created by building up layers of paper and glue over a mould.

Papier mâché is an ancient craft. Soon after the Chinese discovered how to make paper about 2000 years ago, they began to experiment with moulding pieces of paper to make functional and decorative objects. The craft was revived again by the French in the eighteenth century and was used for trays, boxes, and even chairs.

Today commercial papier mâché objects are often glued with epoxy resin which makes them stronger and more durable than items made with the traditional water-soluble glues. Decorative artists use papier mâché to create a hand-carved look at minimal cost. Either buy some of the commercially available papier mâché shapes or mould your own.

PREPARATION

Papier mâché needs no surface preparation. The surface is smooth and already sealed as it is made of paper and glue, a sealer in itself.

DECORATING PROCEDURES

The decorating procedures are the same as for wood (see page 15).

FINISHING

To protect the surface and make cleaning easy, finish with two to four coats of water-based satin or gloss varnish.

BISQUE PORCELAIN

Glazed (shiny) porcelain is not suitable for decorative painting with acrylics. The surface is too glossy to allow the paint to adhere. Bisque porcelain is the kind to use for decorative painting. It is clay which has been fired to maturity but is unglazed.

The surface of bisque porcelain is white and matt in texture, making an ideal base for artists' acrylics. By applying a gloss varnish you can make the finished pieces resemble kiln-fired, glazed ceramics.

PREPARATION

Make sure that the porcelain is smooth and clean. Use a piece of pantihose wrapped over your finger to carefully smooth the surface, if necessary. Remove dust with a soft paintbrush.

DECORATING PROCEDURE

The decorating procedures for porcelain are the same as for wood (see page 15).

FINISHING

You can give the item the look of a fired porcelain piece by varnishing with either water-based gloss varnish or an oil-based gloss varnish such as Watsonia. You will need to use approximately six coats of water-based varnish or two coats of oil-based varnish.

Make sure that the item is free of dust, lint and brush hairs before varnishing, because the gloss finish will show up any faults.

When using the oil-based product, try to leave the paint to cure for two weeks before varnishing. Work outside to avoid nasty fumes. Follow the manufacturer's instructions carefully and make sure that the first coat is thoroughly dry before you apply the second.

Do not use painted porcelain items for food preparation or storage, and do not wash them in a dishwasher. Clean them by wiping with a damp, soapy cloth.

CANDLES
PREPARATION

Apply two coats of all-purpose sealer, allowing each coat to dry thoroughly. The wet sealer softens the wax, so do not touch the candles while they are drying. The wax will, however, become firm again as the sealer dries. Leave the second coat of sealer for 24 hours before decorating.

DECORATING PROCEDURES

Do not base-coat the candle as part of its charm will be the glowing transparent effect of the design when the candle is lit. If you want a coloured background, then buy a coloured candle—black, in particular, looks very sophisticated with a painted design.

Keep your design quick and simple. After all, it is not worth spending hours on something that will simply go up in smoke.

FINISHING

No finishing is needed.

TERRACOTTA

PREPARATION

Submerge the terracotta item in water and allow the water to soak in. Remove the piece from the water, turn it upside down, and place on a towel.

Allow the item to half-dry—it will still be damp but not saturated. Use a sponge brush to apply a coat of all-purpose sealer to the outside of the item. When this coat is thoroughly dry, apply a coat of sealer to the inside. Leave the item to dry for 24 hours before decorating.

DECORATING PROCEDURES

If you do not wish to base-coat the entire surface, choose colours that will look attractive on the terracotta-coloured background. Simple designs are best on terracotta bowls and pots. One of the prettiest pots I have seen was created by a novice folk artist in her seventies, who painted the entire pot antique blue and decorated it with a simple spray of flannel flowers.

A small border design around the rim of a pot is very effective, as is base-coating the rim and saucer and leaving the pot itself the natural terracotta colour. If you are using the terracotta pots inside your home, paint the rim to coordinate with a key colour in your furnishings.

FINISHING

Using a sponge brush, finish with four to six coats of water-based satin or gloss varnish.

Simply wipe the terracotta item, with a damp cloth when necessary. Never wash a painted terracotta piece in the dishwasher.

To prolong the life of your painted pots, do not fill them with soil. Instead use them as 'cache-pots' to hide cheap old pots.

Note: Because sealer has been used on the interior of the item, it should not be used to store or serve food.

GLASS

Glass is not an ideal painting surface because it is so shiny and has little grip to allow good paint adhesion. Traditionally when artists painted designs on windows and glass door panels, they fired them to bake the paint onto the surface. However, you can achieve reasonable results without firing if you use the appropriate products and take care with maintenance of the glass items.

PREPARATION

Clean the glass with Windex and a soft lint-free cloth. Handle the clean glass by the edges to avoid finger smudges.

DECORATING PROCEDURES

Special glass paints and stains that give a very durable finish are available from large art suppliers.

Otherwise, you can use household gloss enamel paint or artists' oil paints or even small tins of modellers' enamels (available from hobby and model-making shops). When using oil paint on glass, use it straight out of the tube and don't add any painting medium.

Acrylic paint is not really suitable for use on glass. Even if you seal the surface first, the paint will rub off very easily or the whole painted area may simply peel off!

FINISHING

No finishing is needed.

Please note that painted designs on glass items—particularly those that are used regularly—will not last indefinitely. If you decorate a set of wine glasses, for instance, you will need to be prepared to touch up the design from time to time. You will, however, prolong the life of the design by handwashing the item carefully. *Never* wash hand-painted glassware in the dishwasher.

LEATHER

Leather hatboxes and trunks are beautiful items to paint with artists' acrylics. You can also paint leather shoes and bags with motifs to match your other clothing. I do, however, recommend that you base-paint the shoes or bag with products available from the shoe section of department stores. If you base-coat shoes with artists' acrylic paint, they will tend to crack with normal wear.

PREPARATION

Have any major repairs to hatboxes or trunks done professionally. Remove hardware, such as hinges and locks, or cover them with masking tape. Wipe the surface clean with a damp cloth. Seal with all-purpose sealer and allow to dry for 24 hours. Then apply at least three or four base coats of artists' acrylics. If you are covering a dark background, you may need to use more coats. Leave each coat to dry thoroughly before applying the next. Wait 24 hours after the last base coat before decorating. This will allow the paint to harden and partially cure.

You can camouflage leather that is slightly dented or damaged, by using a decorative background or finishing technique such as stippling, sponging, crackling, or antiquing. See *The Australian Folk Art Collection* for details.

DECORATING PROCEDURES

The decorating procedures are the same as for wood (see page 15).

FINISHING

Shoes painted with proprietary shoe paints should *not* be varnished.

Finish purely decorative items that will not receive hard wear and tear, with eight to twelve coats of water-based gloss varnish. Make sure that each coat is dry before applying the next. Do not use the item for about a month while the water-based varnish is hardening.

If you plan to use the item regularly (for instance, a hatbox used as luggage), you will need to varnish it with an oil-based product such as Watsonia gloss. About four to six coats should be sufficient. Apply one coat every few days, rubbing lightly between coats with fine steel wool. See 'Sanding' on page 15. Remove any sanding dust, lint, or hairs before applying each coat of varnish.

The oil-based varnish can take several months to cure, so take care with your item during this time as the varnish will not have reached its maximum hardness and durability.

PAPER

Traditionally we think of artists painting on paper and framing their work to hang on the wall. But paper can have a multitude of functional uses as well: for example, hand-painted invitations, greeting cards, stationery, place-cards, or menus.

See page 106 for instructions on how to create embossed lettering for your greeting cards, personalised stationery, and so on.

PREPARATION

There is no special preparation needed. If you plan to paint with watercolours, you should use watercolour paper. And if you intend to use very wet colour washes, the paper will need to be prestretched.

If you like to paint on wood and want to simulate its surface for practice work, try using heavy cardboard available from art suppliers. It can be base-coated and used as a sample board.

DECORATING PROCEDURES

Use your favourite medium for painting on paper: for example, watercolours, acrylics, or soluble watercolour pencils. Experiment with inks and marking pens for liner work.

If you are a folk artist accustomed to working on wood, you will find that paper is far more absorbent. The paint will dry quickly and you will have little time to play with the paint, as you can on less porous surfaces. It is also difficult to remove smudges and mistakes.

Wildflowers look particularly effective if painted with watercolour washes. Add plenty of water to the paint and lightly colour in instead of the usual opaque blocking in. Do not paint over veins or midribs—leave the paper showing beneath.

FINISHING

No special finishing is necessary for functional items.

STATE FLORAL EMBLEMS

Sturt's Desert Rose (Northern Territory)

1

2

3

4

Deborah Kneen
1990

Blue Gum (Tasmania)

1

2

3

STATE FLORAL EMBLEMS

Cooktown Orchid (Queensland)

Royal Bluebell (Australian Capital Territory)

STATE FLORAL EMBLEMS

Sturt's Desert Pea (South Australia)

Mangles' Kangaroo-Paw (Western Australia)

LARGE WILDFLOWERS

Native Passion Flower

1

2

Bower Plant

1

2

Australian Bindweed

1

2

LARGE WILDFLOWERS

Kangaroo Apple

Murray (or Darling) Lily

Guinea Flower

NATIVE DAISIES

Swan River Daisy

1

2

3

Flannel Flower

1

2

3

Ovens Everlasting

1

2

Pink Paper Daisy

1

2

Poached Egg Daisy

1

2

Billy's Buttons

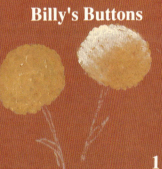
1

2

Golden Everlasting

1

2

Snow Daisy

1 2

CHAPTER 2
DESIGN TIPS

ENLARGING AND REDUCING PATTERNS

Before you enlarge or reduce a pattern to fit a surface, consider whether this is appropriate for the design. If a pattern is too small for the surface and there is excessive space around it, you can try:

- adding a border or band (see page 39);
- taking an element in the existing design and repeating it to increase the size of the design (see page 36).

If the pattern is too large for the surface, you may be able to eliminate some elements from the design while retaining the focal interest. Beware, however, of crowding a design into a limited space.

THE GRID SYSTEM

To enlarge a design in this book using the grid system, trace the design onto tracing paper and rule a border around it. Next rule up a grid over the design. On a sheet of paper with the same dimensions as you want the finished design to be, rule up another enlarged grid. To do this, first count the number of horizontal and vertical rows of squares on the small grid. With a ruler, mark the same number of horizontal and vertical rows of squares on the enlarged grid. Number the horizontal and vertical rows of squares in the original pattern. Then transfer these numbers to the corresponding rows on the enlarged grid. Find a square on the new grid that corresponds to a square on the original. Working one square at a time, use a pencil to mark the enlarged grid with a dot wherever a design line intersects a grid line. Connect the dots by lightly sketching in the contours of the design. Now go over the lines with a felt pen.

If this sounds too tedious and mathematical, take the design to a photocopy or printing shop where special photocopying machines can enlarge and reduce designs by small amounts.

Do, however, observe the laws of copyright. You are welcome to enlarge or reduce the designs in this book by photocopying for your own personal use. But you may need to obtain a publisher's or manufacturer's permission to use designs from other books and sources.

TRANSFERRING PATTERNS

Although I am a firm believer in 'freehanding' designs, I admit that there are times when it is convenient to trace a pattern. When you do trace, keep transfer lines to a minimum. There is no point in transferring fine details—you will only base-paint over those areas anyway when you block in the main colours.

For all surfaces other than fabric:
1. Lay a piece of tracing paper over the pattern and trace it onto the tracing paper.
2. Position the traced pattern on the surface to be painted. Secure with Magic or masking tape if necessary.
3. Lift the traced pattern without disturbing its position and slip a sheet of transfer paper between the pattern and the surface to be painted. Make sure to place the transfer paper with the shiny (impregnated) side against the surface.
4. Use a stylus or empty ballpoint pen to trace over the pattern. You can lift a corner of the transfer paper to check that the design is coming out on the surface and that you are applying sufficient pressure. Trace only the basic pattern, not detailed lines or shading.

Note: Use grey graphite transfer paper when working on a light-coloured background. Use white or light-coloured transfer paper for a dark background. You can buy transfer paper especially designed for fabric (or follow the instructions on page 35).

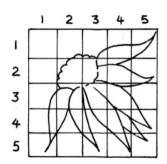

Original flannel flower pattern

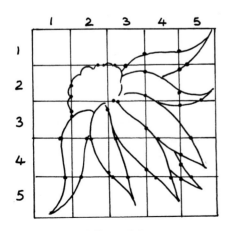

Enlarged flannel flower pattern

Hint: Transfer paper can be used over and over again. Indeed an old sheet is preferable because it does not cause unnecessary smudges. If using a new sheet of transfer paper, rub the shiny side with a piece of paper towel before placing it against the surface.

CORNER MOTIFS

To reverse a corner motif so that it will fit the opposite corner, you should first trace the design onto tracing paper.

Turn the tracing paper over and trace over the design and you will have a reversed motif. If you want to use the design for the bottom corners, simply turn the designs upside down. Note, however, that this is not appropriate for motifs of animals or people.

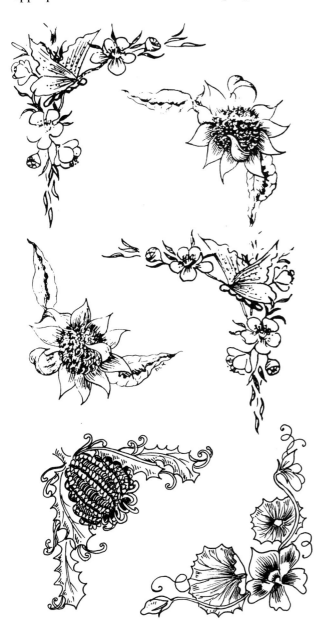

TRANSFERRING DESIGNS TO FABRIC

1. With an ordinary pencil, carefully trace the design outline onto tracing paper. Trace only the minimum lines necessary to guide your painting.
2. Turn the tracing paper over and use a special iron-on transfer pencil to trace over the back of the pattern.
3. Place the tracing paper pattern *transfer pencil side down* on the right side of the fabric and position carefully. Secure with Magic or masking tape to hold the pattern firm and to avoid smudging or smearing the lines.
4. Press over the tracing paper pattern with a warm iron. The heat will transfer the lines to the fabric. When you begin ironing, lift a corner to check that the pattern is transferring properly.

CREATING YOUR OWN DESIGNS

'By viewing Nature,
Nature's handmaid, art,
Makes mighty things from small beginnings grow.'
John Dryden

All artists reach a stage when they want to create their own unique designs. If you have a good feeling for design and colour or natural drawing ability, this will come easily to you. But if you lack confidence, here are some strategies to help you.

Start an 'Ideas Folder' of photos, clippings, greeting cards, and so on, for future use. Look for inspiration from the folder whenever you are stuck for ideas.

Always have a sketchbook and pencil on hand so that you can jot down thoughts or draw interesting subjects.

Examine other people's designs and analyse how they are structured. Determine where the focus of interest is, the shape of the design, how filler flowers are used. Don't just look at the design. Mentally dissect it! What do you like about it? Is there any way you think it could be improved? Would you add anything? Or do you think the design would benefit by being simplified?

In planning your own design, it is important to ask yourself two key questions:

- *What is the function of the item to be painted?*
- *What are its size and shape?*

The design you choose will need to be appropriate to the item's intended use and to its size and shape.

Some pieces such as pretty Victorian-style boxes cry out for elegant floral designs with delicate flowers, ribbons, and lace. A rustic trunk, however, would lend itself to a simple country motif or to stylised folk art flowers. A delicate wine goblet will need an equally delicate border design but would look silly with large flowers covering it. And so on.

Certain traditional items, by their very nature, indicate a certain style. Pieces that are representative of a particular country or region suggest the use of the painting style associated with that locality. For instance, a Norwegian dowry chest brings to mind a Rosemaling style. An Austrian embroidery tine would be perfect decorated with Bauernmalerei motifs.

The shape of the design should enhance the shape of the surface to be painted. This is discussed in some detail on pages 37, 38 and 39. Briefly, the design should fit and follow the shape but not overwhelm it. Leave some space open so that the effect is not overpowering. This open area is known as 'negative space'.

Another point you should consider is the use of colour and any special background or finishing effects. You will obviously paint an item for your home to co-ordinate with the overall colour-scheme.

DESIGN PRINCIPLES

Key principles in any good design are:
- *unity*
- *balance*
- *variety*.

Unity

Unity means that the whole design fits together well, that it is a harmonious composition. The elements in the design should look as though they are meant to be there, not as if they have been thrown together indiscriminately. The simplest way to achieve unity is by repeating elements of the design. For example, one flannel flower may look lonely on the lid of a box. Repeat that flannel flower with a couple of half-opened flowers and a bud or two and you have the makings of a composition. Similarly, you can repeat elements of the design elsewhere on the item. A box with a flannel flower bouquet on the lid, can have some small flannel flowers or buds added on the sides to carry through the motif.

Balance

Balance in a design can be achieved through symmetry (see diagram 1 page 37). But remember that a balanced design does not have to be symmetrical in the exact sense of the word. In achieving balance, the aim is to put an element in one part of your design, and then balance it with something in an opposing area of the design. Filler flowers are an ideal way to balance a floral design (see pages 38 and 51).

Variety

Unity and balance are all very well, but they can make a design boring and static if there is not a little variety. Try varying the sizes and shapes of the design elements (see the diagram below). If you are following the guide curves on page 37, make a few opposing lines that go against the general curve.

These three principles, then, are the technicalities of good design. As you become more experienced, you will automatically take them into account in the design process.

SYMMETRICAL AND ASYMMETRICAL DESIGNS

Symmetrical designs are very ordered and uniform. Some styles of folk art demand symmetry—for instance, Dutch Hinderlooper style and certain types of Rosemaling. These symmetrical styles derived from the Baroque period in decorative art and are always placed in the centre of the surface to be painted.

In developing an Australian style of decorative painting, we can use asymmetrical designs to reflect our casual, relaxed way of life. Australian wildflowers, in particular, are suited to such designs because they thrive at random in the countryside, not in formal European-style gardens. They should not be restricted within the confines of symmetry.

In addition, if you like a touch of the unexpected in designs, you will find asymmetrical compositions more interesting and challenging. They can be adapted to fit any surface because the elements are not a mirror image of each other.

An asymmetrical design will have a focal-point—a definite centre of interest that is usually placed off centre. The other elements in the design should not compete for attention with the focal-point. You can make these other elements smaller or more subdued in colour as they recede from the focus of the design.

Symmetry

Diagram 1

Design Curves

ADDING INTEREST

Little touches add interest. For example, a flower with an odd number of petals tends to look more interesting than one with an even number of petals. Likewise, with an arrangement of leaves, three look better than two, and so on. Experiment with unusual design placement. You could paint a spray of flowers over the lid of a box and continue it down the side. Remember that you do not have to put the design in the centre of the available space.

To put your ideas into practice, cut a piece of tracing paper to the shape of the surface to be painted and doodle with your pencil. I often design around curved lines that are variations of the letters C and S.

Use the curves only as a guide—don't feel confined by them. Sketch in a loose, relaxed fashion and allow elements of the design to veer off a little on either side, but not so much that the curve gets lost.

My final word of advice is *not to overdesign*. The old adage 'less is more' has a lot of truth to it, even in folk art which has a tendency to be 'busy' and cluttered. Remember the importance of negative space.

You will soon develop the judgment to know when to leave well enough alone. If you are undecided about adding a final touch, put the item away for a couple of days, then bring it out and look at it afresh. Always err on the side of simplicity.

THE DESIGN PROCESS

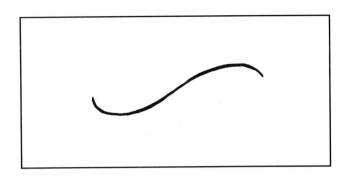

1. Sketch an elongated S curve to suit the rectangular surface.

2. Place the focus of interest (the large flannel flower) just off centre. Give the design a start and a finish, but make the design elements at each end more subdued and muted.

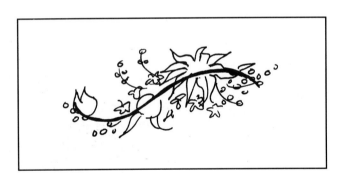

3. Finally add small filler flowers to balance the composition and fill the gaps. Fillers add interest, variety, and movement by creating lines that veer off the main curve. But don't add too many of these or the design will become chaotic.

Wattle and NSW Christmas bush act as 'fillers' for
the main focus of interest, the open flannel flower.

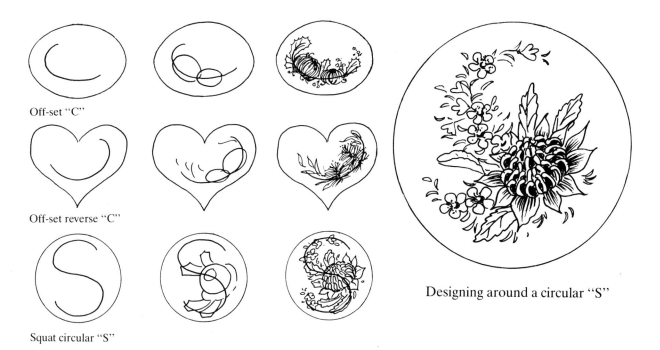

Designing around a circular "S"

Designing around "S" and "C" curves

DESIGNING BORDERS

'I got Thee flowers to strew Thy way.'
George Herbert

For a circular surface, you can experiment with a variety of borders.

(See also pages 97 to 101). If you feel that your design looks unfinished, or lost in a large surface area, the solution is probably to add a border. Borders serve as a trim for the item. They underline and strengthen its shape and contours, and they complement the main design without competing with it.

Choose a border design to suit the style of the piece you have painted. If the main design is simple, the item needs only a plain line or band as a border. To ensure perfect lines along a flat edge, tape down some Magic or masking tape to guide your hand. Remember to mitre the corners of the tape. Before painting, run a knife blade along the edge of the tape to secure it. Carefully remove the tape immediately after painting.

39

You will have to paint curved border lines freehand, and this is not easy unless you have a steady hand. Try to keep your eye just a little ahead of the brush. Some artists find a permanent marking pen easier to control than a brush when painting borders.

Hint: As a precaution apply a thin barrier coat of water-based satin varnish to wood, metal and other appropriate surfaces before painting the line border. Then you can easily remove and repaint any blurred lines.

If you are feeling ambitious, try some of the more detailed borders featured in Chapter 4 or use the techniques outlined below to design your own.

Note: You should always measure the border area and adjust the design so that it fits correctly. Otherwise, if you just go ahead and paint, you may be left with half a flower at the end of the border.

One of the most effective ways of designing a border is to use a wave pattern. Imagine a wave rolling towards the shore and keep the design flowing.

Borders such as these date back to Greco-Roman times and can be found as friezes on walls at Pompeii.

Note: Borders such as those on pages 97 to 101 make delightful designs for bangles.

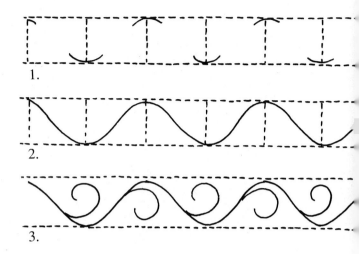

Bangle decorated with a border design

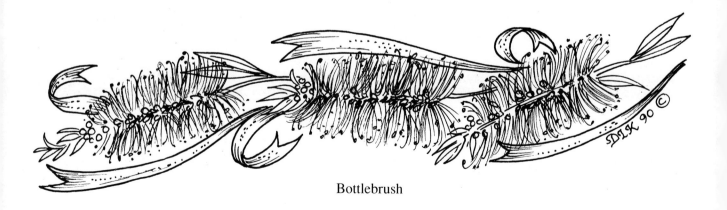

Bottlebrush

CHRISTMAS WILDFLOWERS

Weeping Bottlebrush

1

2

Tropical Banksia

1

2

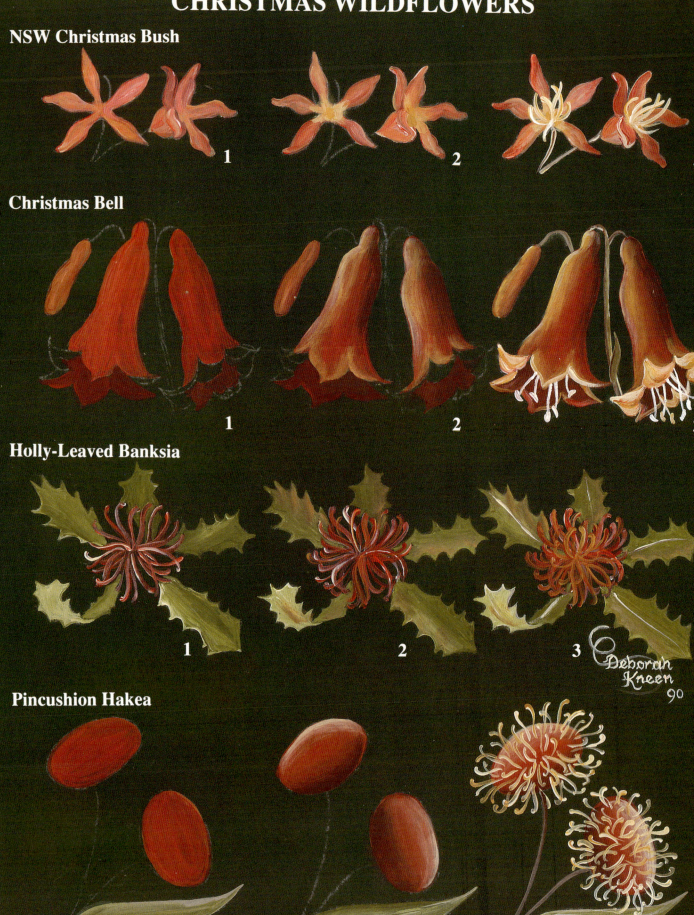

SMALL AND FILLER FLOWERS

SMALL AND FILLER FLOWERS

Heath-Myrtle

Coral Heath

Tree Violet

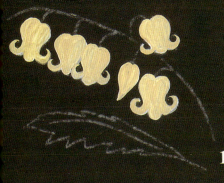  

Peach Blossom Tea Tree   **Maidenhair Fern**

© Deborah Kneen '90

45

BORDERS
See Patterns on pages 97, 98, 100, 101

BORDERS
See patterns on pages 97, 98, 100, 101

47

WILDFLOWER SPRAYS
See pattern on page 79

CHAPTER 3
DESIGNING WITH AUSTRALIAN WILDFLOWERS

USING AUSTRALIAN WILDFLOWERS IN PLACE OF EUROPEAN MOTIFS

Australian native flowers make ideal material for folk art designs. You can use traditional folk art techniques and brushstrokes but the subject-matter will make your designs uniquely Australian.

'Waratah, you are the queen
Of all the flowers to be seen;
Against the sky, glowing red,
A scarlet crown upon your head.'

Isabel Dawes

The waratah could indeed serve as the Australian version of the archetypal folk art rose. Interestingly enough, the rose and the waratah can both be painted from the same basic shape.

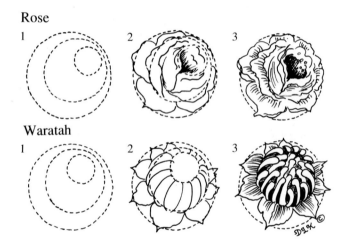

Likewise, the native rosella or Sturt's desert rose, the floral emblem of the Northern Territory (which doesn't look like a rose at all but more like a hibiscus), would be an admirable substitute for the traditional rose.

Sturt's Desert Rose

DAISIES

If you love daisies there are many attractive and colourful native varieties to use in your painting (see page 31). Flannel flowers, too, can be used in place of traditional daisies. I use them frequently because their cheeky faces always add interest to a design. And they are easy to paint. Simply load your brush with a lot of paint and make two shape-following strokes for each petal. The paint will build up along the centre of the petal to create a prominent midrib. (See page 31).

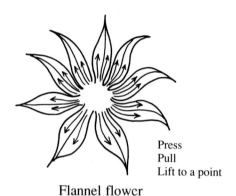

Press
Pull
Lift to a point

Flannel flower

FESTIVE FLOWERS

For festive designs, there are a number of suitable natives: the waratah, bottlebrush, NSW Christmas bush, Christmas bell, holly grevillea, holly-leaved banksia, red-flowering gum, and so on. Gumnuts are an effective replacement for pine-cones. And the leaves of the holly grevillea and the holly-leaved banksia make excellent substitutes for European holly. Native toadstools (*Amanita muscaria*) can replace the traditional German 'Glückpilze' (pronounced 'glook-peel-tser'), the good-luck mushrooms that appear in Bauernmalerei Christmas designs (see pages 32, 41 and 42).

FILLER FLOWERS

European and American folk artists love to use delicate little flowers like lily of the valley and Queen Anne's lace as fillers in their designs. These dainty filler flowers help to balance a composition by filling out gaps in the design. Suitable Australian fillers include our national floral emblem, the wattle, and also NSW Christmas bush, heath myrtle, native clematis, tree violet, native ferns, and so on. (See pages 43 to 45).

And just as you would add foliage to a real flower arrangement to make it look full and balanced, you can add leaves such as dryandra and eucalypt to your painted arrangements.

So, for most European flowers used in traditional folk art, there is an Australian counterpart that is just as attractive. On the next page there is a quick reference table with some commonly used European floral motifs and suggested Australian equivalents. If you have an existing European or American design, you can then adapt it for Australian native flowers.

Holly

Holly grevillea

Glückpilze

Native toadstools

Christmas Look-Alikes

Wattle

NSW Christmas bush

Maidenhair fern

Fillers

51

FAVOURITE FLORAL MOTIFS (Conversion Table)

European/North American		Australian	
Berries (e.g. strawberries, raspberries)		Queensland Bramble	
Crabapple	Dark red	Wombat Berry	orange
Foxglove		Native Foxglove	purple
Hollyhock		Australian Hollyhock	
Lily of the Valley		Tree Violet	
Morning Glory		Australian Bindweed	
Peach Blossom		Peach Blossom Tea-Tree	
Tulip		Flannel Flower Bud	
Violet		Native Violet	

A BASIC DRAWING AND PAINTING GUIDE TO FORTY AUSTRALIAN WILDFLOWERS

*'See how the flowers, as at parade,
Under their colours stand display'd.'*
Andrew Marvell

The table on the following pages is a quick guide to sketching and painting a sample of Australian wildflowers.

This table is intended for the decorative and folk artist rather than the botanical illustrator. A *botanical* artist has to present a plant portrait that is both artistically appealing and able to sustain critical scientific analysis. This is achieved by undertaking field trips to collect specimens and then assiduously copying them in the studio. Such analysis is beyond the aims and scope of decorative and folk painting.

The *decorative* artist, on the other hand, aims to capture an overall impression of the flower. She often works from her imagination, which enables her to capture the essence of the plant rather than all its realistic details.

The *folk* artist takes the impressionistic approach even further than the decorative artist. She bases her work on a simple peasant tradition and sometimes her painted flowers will be so stylised that they bear little resemblance to the real thing. She may even paint several different species of flower growing on the one stem. Or she may disregard proportion and depict a flower towering over a human figure.

As I said in the Preface, it is a matter of personal choice whether you adopt a decorative or a folk painting approach. You can be quite free in your interpretation and you don't need to be overly concerned about proportion—in the world of folk art, a waratah can be the same size as a flannel flower if that suits your design and purpose. I do suggest, however, you do not take artistic licence too far in terms of colour. Don't paint blue flannel flowers or yellow waratahs!

The table is organised according to levels of painting difficulty. This is a fairly subjective judgment on my part, but it will give you some idea of whether you will be able to master a particular flower in the light of your current painting ability. Do remember, however, that even a difficult flower like the waratah can be simplified and stylised so that it is suitable for a beginner.

KEY TO TABLES
Key to Level of Painting Difficulty

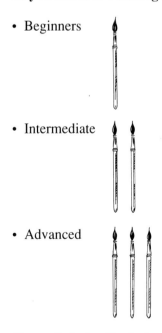

- Beginners

- Intermediate

- Advanced

Key to Painting Techniques

B = base colour   H = highlight
S = shading   LW = liner work

Botanical native violet   Folk art native violet

Common and Botanical Names	Level of Painting Difficulty	Basic Flower Shape and Details
Australian Bindweed *Convolvulus erubescens*	2 brushes	green, pink
Blue Gum *Eucalyptus globulus*	2 brushes	brown with cream LW, nuts
Bower Plant *Pandorea jasminoides*	2 brushes	trumpet-shaped 5 petals at end of trumpet
Brown Boronia *Boronia megastigma*	1 brush	cup-shaped
Christmas Bell *Blandfordia grandiflora*	3 brushes	flowers clustered at top of tall stalk

Flower Base Colour(s)	Flower Shading and Highlight Details	Basic Leaf Shape and Details	Leaf Base—Shading and Highlight Details
Dusty pink	S: Dark pink along pleats and edges. H: Pale pink on centre of petals. Cream centre. LW: Pale green stamens.		B: Pine green. S: Dark green. H: Pale green underside. LW: White veins.
Pale yellow. Use dry brush-strokes. Centre: light green circle. Cap: grey-green.	S: Dark brown semi-circle at edge of centre. H: Cream dry overstrokes. LW: Cream dots around edge.		B: Pine green. S: Dark green, brown. H: Grey midrib and veins.
Pale pink	S: Red centre of throat, deepening to very dark brown. H: White at centre and edges of petals.	curved pointed tip	B: Pine green. S: Brownish-green. H: Pale green. LW: Pale green midrib.
Petals: yellow on inside; brown on outside. Centre: diamond-shaped yellow-orange.	S: Dark brown at base of brown petals. H: White at edge of yellow petals. LW: Brown dots around diamond at centre.	small narrow leaves	B: Light green. LW: Outline with pine green.
Tomato red	S: Dark red to brown inside bell. H: Yellow tips. LW: Long white stamens.	stalk, tall strappy leaves	B: Pine green. S: Dark green. H: Yellow-green.

Common and Botanical Names	Level of Painting Difficulty	Basic Flower Shape and Details
Cooktown Orchid *Dendrobium bigibbum*	🖌🖌🖌	petals overlap — 3 pointed petals, 2 round petals, sack-shaped
Flannel Flower *Actinotus helianthi*	🖌🖌	approximately 10 petals when fully open; bud
Golden Wattle *Acacia pycnantha*	🖌	fluffy balls
Guinea Flower *Hibbertia dentata*	🖌🖌	
Heath-Myrtle *Micromyrtus ciliata*	🖌	5 outer petals, 5 small inner petals

Flower Base Colour(s)	Flower Shading and Highlight Details	Basic Leaf Shape and Details	Leaf Base—Shading and Highlight Details
Dusty pink	S: Dark pink to burgundy near sack and where petals overlap. Centre: Dark brown. H: Pale pink to white at edges of petals.	thin strappy leaves	B: Dark green. S: Black green. H: Pale green to white along centre of leaf.
Cream Petals painted in 2 shape-following strokes—allow the paint to build up along the centre of each petal to form a midrib.	S: Diluted teal green wash on centre and at base of petals. LW: Diluted teal green petal tips. Teal green dots on centre.	comma strokes	B: White with a little teal green. H: White.
Yellow	S: Mustard comma stroke. H: White comma stroke on other side of each ball. LW: Fine white lines around each ball.	long narrow leaves with prominent midrib	B: Double-loaded brown and yellow-green. LW: Grey midrib.
Pale yellow	S: Dark yellow at base of petals and where they overlap. H: White at centre of petals. LW: Yellow dots in centre.		B: Pine green. S: Brownish-green along midrib and veins. LW: Pale green veins.
White	S: Dark pink centre frill. Leave centre circle white. Dark pink at base of buds.	numerous small pointed leaves	B: Pine green. S: Dark green outline. H: Touch of pale green on centre of leaf.

Common and Botanical Names	Level of Painting Difficulty	Basic Flower Shape and Details
Holly Grevillea *Grevillea ilicifolia*	🖌🖌	
Kangaroo Apple *Solanum aviculare*	🖌🖌	5 long stamens; 5 petals with fluted edges
Kangaroo Paw *Anigozanthos manglesii*	🖌🖌	light green tubes; red tips; red stalk
Leatherwood *Eucryphia lucida*	🖌	4 overlapping rounded petals; many stamens
Lilly Pilly *Waterhousea floribunda*	🖌🖌	berries

Flower Base Colour(s)	Flower Shading and Highlight Details	Basic Leaf Shape and Details	Leaf Base—Shading and Highlight Details
Red styles with yellow dots on end. Lower dots are light green.	S: Dark green on one side of each lower dot. LW: Outline lower dots in dark green.		B: Pine green S: Black-green H: Pale green to white. LW: Pale grey midrib and veins.
Mauve	S: Violet around centre and fluted edges. H: White along pleat lines. LW: Violet line down centre of each petal. Long yellow stamens.	long pointed leaves	B: Grey-green. S: Dark green along centre. LW: Yellow-green midrib and veins.
Red stem. Light green tubes with a red dot at end.	S: Brown on one side of stem. Dark green on tubes. H: Touch of light green on tubes. LW: Fine black-green lines on tubes.	long strappy leaves	B: Grey-green. H: Pale grey.
White	LW: Grey stamens. Black dots at end of stamens.	oval leaves	B: Pale green. S: Pine green. LW: Pale grey midrib. Pale green stem.
Flowers: White centre. Scratchy white strokes for flower petals. Fruit: Pale green double-loaded with a touch of purple.	S: Underside of centre dark cream. LW: White dots on flowers.	large pointed leaves light brown stem	B: Pine green. S: Dark green. H: Touches of pale green. LW: Pale green to white midrib and veins.

Common and Botanical Names	Level of Painting Difficulty	Basic Flower Shape and Details
Murray Lily *Crinum flaccidum*	1 brush	6 stamens, 6 pointed petals
Native Clematis *Clematis aristata*	1 brush	four narrow pointed petals
Native Daphne *Eriostemon myoporoides*	2 brushes	5 large pointed petals, yellow dots, centre in close-up, bud is pink, woody stems
Native Fuchsia *Correa reflexa*	2 brushes	brown cap, white tips, small bell-shaped flowers, 8 stamens
Native Rosella *Hibiscus heterophyllus*	3 brushes	5 overlapping pleated petals, centre column with stamens at top

Flower base Colour(s)	Flower Shading and Highlight Details	Basic Leaf Shape and Details	Leaf Base—Shading and Highlight Details
White	S: Cream. LW: Cream stamens with tiny yellow dots at top.		B: Pine green. S: Dark green. H: White. LW: Dark green midrib.
Cream Round yellow centre.	LW: Profusion of fine yellow stamens.		B: Pale green. S: Pine green. LW: Pale grey midrib and veins.
Flowers: White. Buds: Pink with a touch of yellow. Stems: Double-loaded grey and brown.	S: Yellow at base of petals. LW: Yellow dots in centre.		B: Pine green with a touch of teal green. H: Pale green. LW: Pale grey to white midrib.
Red	S: Dark red to brown on one side. H: White tips. LW: Long yellow stamens.	broad, heart-shaped leaves	B: Pine green. H: Smudge on a touch of brown and Norwegian orange. LW: Dark brown veins.
Double-loaded coral and white strokes.	S: Deep salmon pink deepening to dark brown at centre. H: White on centres of petals. LW: Cream central column and stamens.	long, narrow pointed leaves	B: Pine green. S: Brownish-green. H: As for native fuchsia. LW: Pale grey midrib and veins.

Common and Botanical Names	Level of Painting Difficulty	Basic Flower Shape and Details
Native Violet *Viola hederacea*	🖌️🖌️	darkest purple — bud 5 petals, the lowest petal is broadest — profile
NSW Christmas bush *Ceratopetalum gummiferum*	🖌️	tiny flowers with 5 petals
Ovens Everlasting Daisy *Helichrysum stirlingii*	🖌️	small button-shaped flowers with large centres
Peach Blossom Tea-Tree *Leptospermum squarrosum*	🖌️	5 round petals, many stamens
Pincushion Hakea *Hakea laurina*	🖌️🖌️	

Flower Base Colour(s)	Flower Shading and Highlight Details	Basic Leaf Shape and Details	Leaf Base—Shading and Highlight Details
White	S: Mauve at base of petal. Purple across centre of each petal. LW: Yellow dot at centre. Purple lines on petal.	circular leaves with serrated edges; upturned leaf; pale green on underside	B: Pine green. S: Dark green. LW: Light green veins.
Reddish-pink	H: Pale pink to white at base of petals. LW: Yellow stamens at centre.	3 leaves in a set; narrow, pointed leaves with serrated edges	B: Yellow-green. H: Smudge on a touch of Norwegian orange. LW: Brown midrib.
Petals: White Centre: Brown	S: Dark brown at base of centre. LW: Dark brown dots on centre.	long, narrow leaves	B: Pine green. S: Dark green. LW: Pale green midrib and veins.
Pale pink petals Pale green centre	S: Dark pink at base of petals. LW: Dark pink to burgundy stamens.	tiny, narrow, pointed leaves	B: Yellow-green. LW: Outline some of the leaves with pine green.
Orange-red circle	S: Float brown on one side of circle H: Float yellow on other side of circle LW: A profusion of fine cream stamens.	long, pointed leaves; 3 vertical veins	B: Grey-green. S: Pine green and brown. LW: Pale yellow green vertical veins. Brown stems.

Common and Botanical Names	Level of Painting Difficulty	Basic Flower Shape and Details
Pink Heath *Epacris impressa*	◆◆	bell-shaped flowers
Poached Egg Daisy *Myriocephalus stuartii*	◆◆	button-shaped flowers large yellow centre
Red-Flowering Gum *Eucalyptus ficifolia*	◆◆	pale green cap grey brown gumnuts
River Buttercup *Ranunculus inundatus*	◆	5 rounded petals flowers on long stalks
Rock Orchid *Dendrobium speciosum*	◆◆	centre close-up

Flower Base Colour(s)	Flower Shading and Highlight Details	Basic Leaf Shape and Details	Leaf Base—Shading and Highlight Details
Bluish purple.	H: A touch of white at base of each petal. LW: Dark purple line down centre of each petal. Yellow stamens in centre.	long leaves with serrated edges	B: Pine green. H: Yellow-green.
Yellow-orange. Use dry scratchy brushstrokes.	S: Add some strokes of Norwegian orange, particularly at the base and top.	long, narrow leaves with triangular points	B: Pine green. LW: White midrib.
Bright red petals. Black spot at centre of each petal.	S: Dark red to brown near black spot. H: White on petal tips. White highlight on each black spot.		B: Grey-green. LW: Fine brownish green hairs around each leaf.
Double-loaded white and pale pink.	S: Dark red to deep burgundy at centre. H: White strokes on petals. LW: Stamen column is double-loaded white and burgundy.		B: Dark green. LW: Grey-green midribs and veins.
Pinkish mauve petals. Yellow centre.	S: Dark pink to burgundy at base of petals. H: Pale pink to white on petal tips. LW: Norwegian orange dots on centre.	fine leaves	LW: Fine leaves painted pine green.

67

Common and Botanical Names	Level of Painting Difficulty	Basic Flower Shape and Details
Tree Violet *Hymenanthera dentata*	2 brushes	sepals — 5 tiny curled petals (2 hidden)
Tropical Banksia *Banksia dentata*	2 brushes	banksia 'man' brown with dark brown shading and liner work
Waratah *Telopea speciosissima*	3 brushes	tubular with rounded tip bracts
Weeping Bottlebrush *Callistemon macropunctatus*	2 brushes	
White Paper Daisy *Helichrysum elatum*	2 brushes	numerous pointed petals in layers bud

Flower Base Colour(s)	Flower Shading and Highlight Details	Basic Leaf Shape and Details	Leaf Base—Shading and Highlight Details
Cream flowers. Pale green sepals.	LW: Outline some of the tiny curled petals with pale grey.	many long, narrow, serrated leaves	B: Pine green. H: Pale green. LW: Dark green mid-rib and veins.
Cylindrical flowers created with dry scratchy brushstrokes of yellow-orange.	S: Add some strokes of Norwegian orange.	broader at tip; long wedge-shaped leaves with sharply serrated edges	B: Grey-green. S: Pine green. LW: White midrib.
Block in basic shape with bright red. Make sure to use shape-following strokes for the bracts.	S: Reddish-brown at base of globe and bracts. H: Yellow to white on tips of bracts. LW: Double-loaded red and white stamens on globe.		B: Pine green. S: Dark green at base. H: Touch of yellow-green. LW: Pale grey veins.
Paint cylindrical flowers with dry scratchy brushstrokes of dark red.	S: Dark brown dots in centre of cylinder. LW: Yellow dots scattered all over cylinder.	sharp point; pale brown nuts with dark brown centres	B: Grey-green. LW: White midrib.
White petals. Yellow centre.	S: Pale grey at base of petals. LW: Dots of Norwegian orange on centre.	long, narrow leaves; grey stem	B: Grey-green. S: Pine green.

FACTS ABOUT THE WILDFLOWERS

AUSTRALIAN BINDWEED
The native bindweed is a climber that resembles the ubiquitous exotic morning glory vine.

BLUE GUM
This tree, the floral emblem of Tasmania, has clusters of fluffy yellow-cream flowers.

BORONIA
Named after an Italian botanist, Francesco Borone, this small shrub with fragrant leaves has many varieties and colours, including pink, brown, and yellow.

BOWER PLANT
Similar to the Wonga vine, this climber with pink trumpet flowers is now a popular plant in nurseries.

CHRISTMAS BELL
Native to the heathlands of the east coast and Tasmania, the Christmas Bell is a red and yellow bell-shaped lily that flowers in the summer months.

COOKTOWN ORCHID
The floral emblem of Queensland, this pink orchid grows on rocks and trees in Queensland forests.

FLANNEL FLOWER
So-named because of its woolly textured petals, the flannel flower grows in sandy areas of New South Wales and Queensland, where it flowers through the summer months.

GUINEA FLOWER
The showy guinea flower, which grows in all States, can be found as a small plant, shrub, or vine.

HEATH MYRTLE
A shrub with many small pink and white flowers, the heath myrtle is found in the heathlands of the east coast and South Australia.

HOLLY GREVILLEA
A low-growing shrub with prickly leaves and fine red tube-like flowers, the holly grevillea is found in the scrublands of southern Australia.

KANGAROO APPLE
A shrub with attractive purple flowers, the kangaroo apple grows in the east coast rainforests.

KANGAROO PAW
The floral emblem of Western Australia, Mangle's kangaroo paw is a plant with long stems topped by green and red finger-like flowers.

LEATHERWOOD
The leatherwood tree, which grows in the forests of Victoria and Tasmania, has perfumed white flowers.

LILLY PILLY
A tree with white fluffy flowers and greenish-purple berries, the lilly pilly is found beside creeks and rivers in eastern Australia.

MURRAY LILY
Also known as the Darling lily, this white flower grows in the wetlands in all States.

NATIVE CLEMATIS
A climber with white star-like flowers, the native clematis grows in the eastern States.

NATIVE DAPHNE
This shrub with beautiful, white waxy flowers grows in the eastern States.

NATIVE FUCHSIA
The small red and white bell-shaped flowers of this shrub appear in winter and spring.

NATIVE ROSELLA
Resembling a hibiscus, the native rosella is a small tree with white, pink, or yellow flowers and edible fruits that are used to make jam.

NATIVE VIOLET
This dainty ground-cover has small purple and white flowers on fine erect stems.

NSW CHRISTMAS BUSH
This small tree with its summer mantle of tiny red flowers was indiscriminately cut down by the early colonists for Christmas floral arrangements. It became a rarity in the bush but survives as a popular garden feature.

OVENS EVERLASTING DAISY
As their name suggests, these small button-shaped daisies can be dried and preserved. They grow in the Alps of New South Wales and Victoria.

PEACH BLOSSOM TEA-TREE
This shrub, with its pink blossoms and brown 'nuts', grows in the sandy areas of New South Wales.

PINCUSHION HAKEA
Resembling a red pincushion with cream pins stuck into it, the flowers of this tree appear in the cooler months in Western Australia.

PINK HEATH
Also known as 'common heath', Victoria's floral emblem is a plant with tall stems and clusters of pinkish-red bell-shaped flowers.

POACHED EGG DAISY
These tall button-shaped daisies flower profusely in the warmer months in arid countryside.

RED-FLOWERING GUM
 This tree, loaded in summer with fluffy red flowers, is native to Western Australia.

RIVER BUTTERCUP
 The native buttercup flowers in spring and summer in the wetlands of the eastern States.

ROCK ORCHID
 This fragrant yellow orchid, which grows on rocks and trees in the eastern States, flowers from autumn to spring.

ROYAL BLUEBELL
 The last State floral emblem to be proclaimed, this richly coloured bluebell grows in the Southern Alps.

SHOWY DRYANDRA
 The yellow globe-like flowers of the dryandra and its collar of spiky leaves make it ideal for drying and preserving. It is native to Western Australia.

STURT'S DESERT PEA
 The floral emblem of South Australia, this desert plant with its red petals and shiny black 'boss' was first collected by William Dampier, the seventeenth-century explorer, and later rediscovered by Charles Sturt.

STURT'S DESERT ROSE
 A shrub with pink hibiscus-like flowers, the floral emblem of the Northern Territory also grows in the arid areas of the other mainland States.

SWAN RIVER DAISY
 This blue or purple-pink daisy flowers for much of the year in central Australia.

TREE VIOLET
 With tiny cream bell-like flowers crowded on its stems, this tree grows in the wetlands of the southern States.

TROPICAL BANKSIA
 A shrub with wiry yellow cylinder-shaped flowers and spiky leaves, the tropical banksia flowers in the cooler months. It is native to the wetlands of the Northern Territory.

WARATAH
 The floral emblem of New South Wales bears globe-like red flowers on tall stems.

WATTLE
 The national floral emblem, this tree is loaded with small fluffy yellow balls in late winter.

WEEPING BOTTLEBRUSH
 This shrub, with flower spikes resembling cylindrical brushes, is native to New South Wales and Queensland.

WHITE PAPER DAISY
 The profuse papery petals of this daisy lend themselves to drying. It flowers in spring in eastern Australia.

Golden Everlasting

CHAPTER 4
WILDFLOWER PATTERNS

Cover Design featuring Waratahs, Flannel Flowers, Bottlebrush and Wattle.

See Colour Worksheet page 81

Guinea Flower

Waratahs, Banksia "men" and Billy's Buttons

Cooktown Orchids and Royal Bluebells

Hibiscus Spray
Lovely on a T-shirt

Flannel Flower and Wattle Spray

Native Violets

Scarlet Banksia

Guinea Flower, Swan River Daisies, Billy's Buttons

See Colour Worksheet page 82

78 Native Passion Flower Trellis

See back cover

NATIVE PASSION FLOWER TRELLIS
See pattern on page 78

HOMESTEAD WREATH
See pattern on page 90

WARATAH BABIES
See pattern on page 96

ROSELLA BRIDE
See pattern on page 93

WILDFLOWER ADVENT TREE
See pattern on pages 94 and 95

WILDFLOWER ALPHABET
See pattern on page 105

Wildflower Clock

See Colour Worksheet page 83

Landscape Wreath featuring Flannel Flowers, Wattle, Native Fuschia

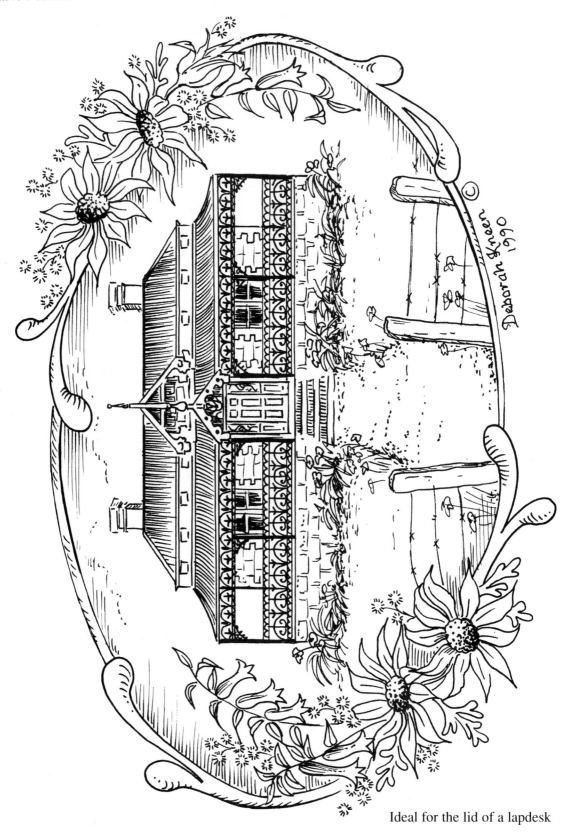

Ideal for the lid of a lapdesk

Wildflower Garden featuring Christmas Bells, Sturt's Desert Pea, Flannel Flowers and Ovens Everlasting.

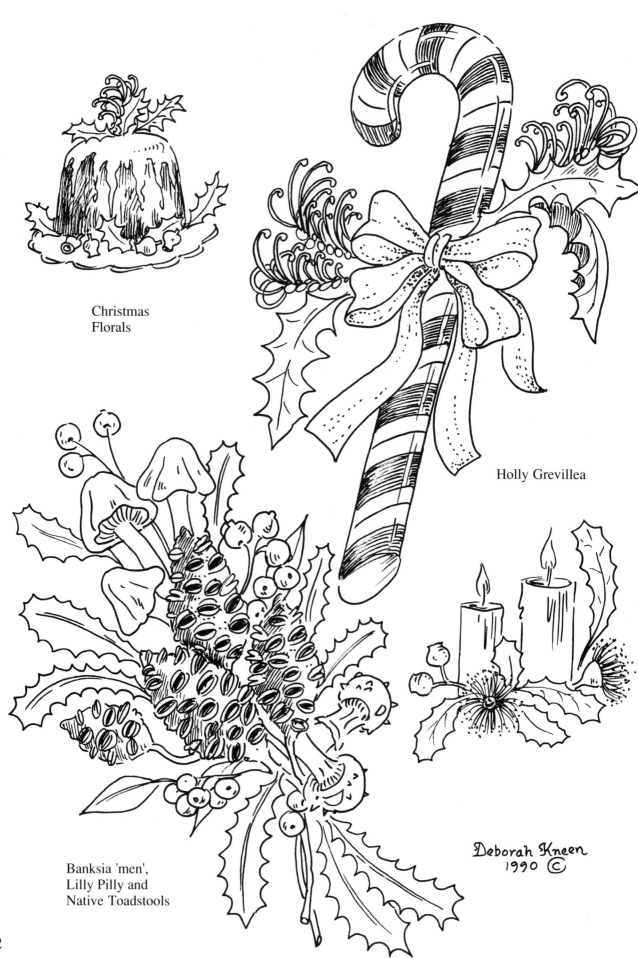

Christmas Florals

Holly Grevillea

Banksia 'men',
Lilly Pilly and
Native Toadstools

Deborah Kneen
1990 ©

See Colour Worksheet page 85

Rosella Bride

See Colour Worksheet pages 86 and 87

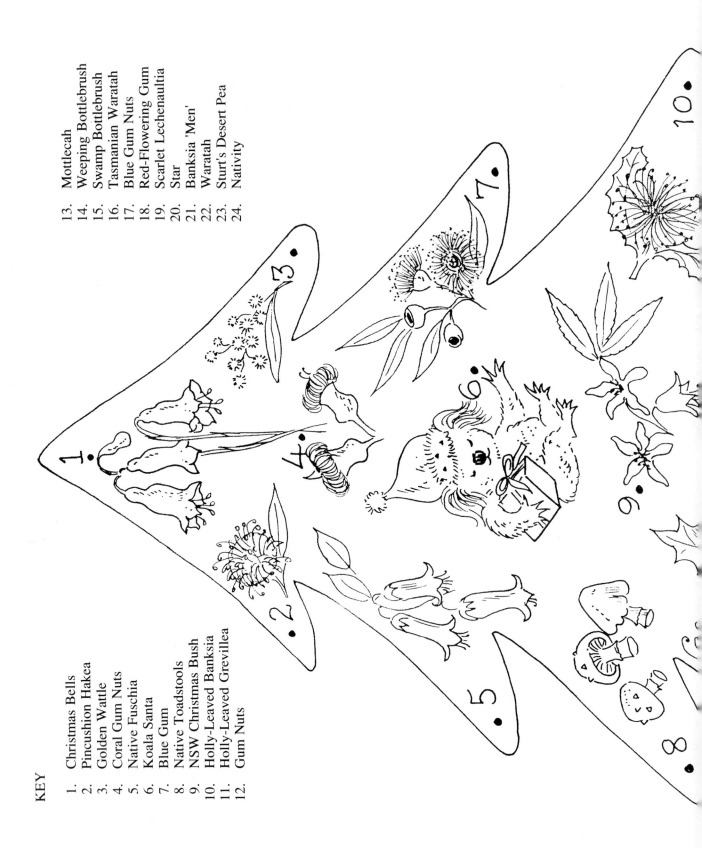

KEY
1. Christmas Bells
2. Pincushion Hakea
3. Golden Wattle
4. Coral Gum Nuts
5. Native Fuschia
6. Koala Santa
7. Blue Gum
8. Native Toadstools
9. NSW Christmas Bush
10. Holly-Leaved Banksia
11. Holly-Leaved Grevillea
12. Gum Nuts
13. Mottlecah
14. Weeping Bottlebrush
15. Swamp Bottlebrush
16. Tasmanian Waratah
17. Blue Gum Nuts
18. Red-Flowering Gum
19. Scarlet Lechenaultia
20. Star
21. Banksia 'Men'
22. Waratah
23. Sturt's Desert Pea
24. Nativity

Australian Advent Tree–cut from Craftwood and slot into a stand. Attach 24 small brass cup hooks and hang a lolly from each. Children take a lolly for each day of Advent–December 1 to December 24. Note: December 6 is St. Nicholas' Day and traditionally is represented by a Santa figure. December 24 always features the Nativity.

See Colour Worksheet page 84

Waratah Babies

Baby or Christening motifs–
suitable for a plate, box, name plaque,
clock, nursery furniture and linen, ...

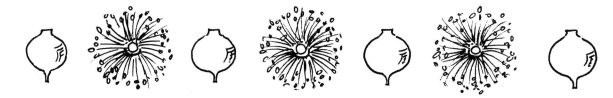

Lilly Pilly Border

Gum Blossom Border

Gum Nut Border

Leatherwood Border

Waratah Basket Border

Peach Blossom Tea Tree Border

Wattle Border

Wonga Vine Border

Bower Plant Border

Kangaroo Apple Border

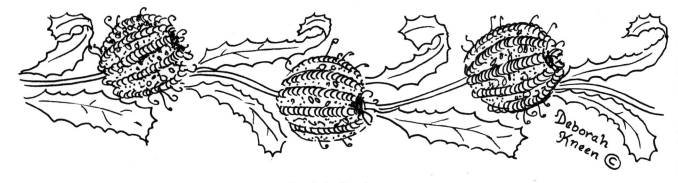

Banksia Border

Native Daisy Border

Waratah Border

Cooktown Orchid Border

Sturt's Desert Pea Border

Christmas Bush Border

Ovens Everlasting Border

Waratah Border

Native Violet Border

Royal Bluebell Border

Queensland Bramble Border

Holly Grevillea Border

Boronia Border

Guinea Flower Border

Native Fern Border

River Buttercup Border

Flannel Flower Border

Bower Plant

APPENDIX

LETTERING AND NUMERALS

There are many occasions when you will want to give a personal touch to an item by painting an inscription, a verse, a name, or a date. You don't need to be a skilled calligrapher to obtain professional results.

If you want to do your own lettering, consult any of the excellent books on the subject. Remember to treat lettering as liner work and to mix your paint to the consistency of Indian ink. Or you can cheat and use a permanent marking pen (or a fabric paint pen for fabric).

One of the most suitable styles of lettering for our purposes is italics (see diagram 1). It is a relatively easy style to master and one that looks effective with folk art designs.

Diagram 1

Whatever style of lettering you decide to use, you will need to design it carefully. First cut a piece of tracing paper to the size of the surface. Then rule up guidelines for the base, lower case, and capitals (see diagram 2). Roughly sketch the letters, adjusting them until they look right. Some letters (e.g. M and W) take up more space than other letters so don't leave equal space for each letter. If you have more than one word, allow plenty of space between words so that they do not run into each other visually. Also remember to leave plenty of space above and below the lettering. Don't crowd it into the available space. If the lettering looks cramped, rub it out and reduce the size of the letters by ruling new guidelines.

When you are happy with the effect, centre the tracing paper on the surface and transfer the letters with transfer paper and a stylus.

Guidelines:

Diagram 2

CHEATING WITH LETTERING

For many artists, however, lettering is truly daunting, so here are some short cuts for the faint-hearted.

You can make use of ready-made lettering and number stencils, available from newsagents and art suppliers. For best results, use a dry stencil brush and very little paint. Wipe most of the paint off the brush and onto a paper towel before stencilling.

Commercial pressed-type alphabets and numerals such as Letraset offer a wide range of fonts and sizes. They are ideal for applying to paper and hard surfaces like wood and metal. You can conceal their origins by painting over the letters with a liner brush in a colour to complement the item on which you are working. This will soften the commercial letters and give the impression that you have painted them yourself. For extra depth and effect, you may wish to paint fine shadow outlines around the letters. Do this with a liner brush or a fine-point permanent marking pen. Shadow outlines create a three-dimensional effect but remember to be consistent with your shadowing. See diagram 3. If you have used pressed-type letters on wood, metal, etc, they can be varnished.

Diagram 3

KEY TO WILDFLOWER ALPHABET
Australian Bindweed
Blue Gum
Cooktown Orchid
Dendrobium speciosum
Eucryphia lucida
Flannel Flower
Guinea Flower
Heath Myrtle
Ironbark
Juniper Wattle
Kangaroo Paw
Lilly Pilly
Minnie Daisy
Native Violet
Ovens Everlasting
Pink Heath
Queensland Bramble
Royal Bluebell
Sturt's Desert Rose
Tropical Banksia
Umbrella Fern
Tree Violet
Waratah
Xanthorrhoea australis
Yellow Hakea
Zieria

See Colour Worksheet page 88

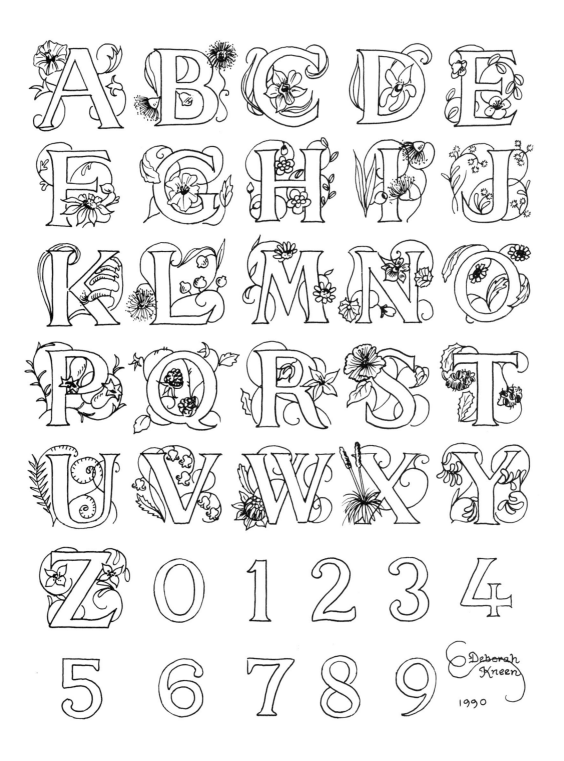

A wildflower alphabet

EMBOSSED LETTERING

An elegant method of lettering on paper is to create raised or embossed letters.

Use the plastic letter stencils mentioned earlier and the paper of your choice. Normal sheets of stationery or even lightweight watercolour or pastel paper give excellent results but thick paper such as cardboard is too difficult to emboss.

You will need an embossing tool (also known as a 'burnishing tool')—available from art suppliers—or you can substitute a knitting needle (use the point) or a potato peeler (use the pointed, curved end) or the wooden end of a fine paint brush.

Place the stencil *reverse side down* on a light-box or against a well-lit window. Put the paper on top of the stencil. Make sure that each letter is placed correctly before you emboss it. Remember that you will be looking at the letters back to front. Use the embossing tool or equivalent to press firmly around the edge of each letter. When you turn the paper over, raised letters will be revealed.

You can leave the letters unadorned or paint pale colour washes over them with watercolour paint or thinned acrylic.

CLOCK FACES

For clock faces, you can use pressed-type numerals or buy brass numerals to glue onto the surface.

Historical Note: You may have wondered about the use of the numeral IIII on clock faces, instead of the correct Roman symbol IV. The symbol IIII is indeed standard and correct on clocks. It is a clock-making tradition for which two explanations are given: it is a matter of symmetry (to offset the VIII), or the dictate of a French king.

Cooktown Orchid

USEFUL ADDRESSES

Alderson's Craft Mart, 264 Railway Parade, Kogarah, NSW 2217.
(02) 587 2699

Artisan Hobby Ceramics, 36 Townsville Street, Fyshwick, ACT 2609.
(062) 806673

Boronia Arts-Crafts, 246 Dorset Road, Boronia, Vic. 3155.
(03) 762 1751

Broughton Cottage Folk Art, 3A Page Street, Wentworthville, NSW 2145.
(02) 631 1946

Clare House Folk Art, 401 Whites Road, Ohoka Kaiapoi RD2, New Zealand.
(502) 26514

Country Lane Collectables, P.O. Box 501, Plympton SA 5038
(08) 378 3102

Creative Characters Wood 'n Tole, 33 Tallebudgera Road, West Burleigh, Qld. 4218.

Elsa's Folk Art Studio, 12 Myrtle Street, Normanhurst, NSW 2076.
(02) 484 5447

The Folk Art Studio, 178 Sydney Road, Fairlight, NSW 2094.
(02) 949 7818

Folklore House, 186 Latrobe Terrace, Paddington, Qld 4064.
(07) 368 1027

The Foster Folk Studio, Shop 5, 18 Alma Road, New Lambton, NSW 2305.
(049) 528 528

From Lois With Love, 311 Elizabeth Street, Hobart, Tas. 7000
(002) 345 469

Gloucester Heritage Crafts, "Rochelle", RMB 131 Fairbairns Lane, Gloucester, NSW 2422.
(065) 581 528

Heather Phillips Folk Art Studio, 6A Station Street, Toowoomba, Qld. 4350.
(076) 32 1177

Janet's Art Supplies, 145 Victoria Avenue, Chatswood, NSW 2067.
(02) 417 8572

Mountain Living, 17 Station Street, Wentworth Falls, NSW 2782.
(047) 571818

Nancraft, 289 Elizabeth Street, Melbourne, Vic. 3000.
(03) 670 6222

Native Plants, 155 Taren Point Road, Taren Point, NSW 2229.
(02) 526 1533

Pauline's Crafts and Folk Art Supplies, 8 Montifiore Street, Launceston, Tas. 7250.
(003) 443 806

The Porcelain Arts Centre, 14 Moore Avenue, West Lindfield, NSW 2070.
(02) 416 6428

Timber Turn Woodturners and Manufacturers, 1 Shepley Avenue, Panorama, SA 5041.
(08) 277 5056

Will's Quills, 164 Victoria Avenue, Chatswood, NSW 2067.
(02) 411 2500

Woolbrook Cottage Crafts, Balmoral Road, Cavendish, Vic. 3408.
(055) 74 2287

NOTE: Many of these businesses offer mail order services.

METAL PREPARATION

The Aquatrol Company (makers of Penetrol),
31 Hugh Street, Belmore, NSW 2192.
(02) 759 2389 or (008) 226 113

FURTHER READING

Here are some helpful books that will guide and inspire you with theory, ideas, techniques, tips, and general reference material. If you work on one particular surface, such as fabric, don't dismiss books on, say, wood or porcelain painting. They will often contain designs and ideas that you can adapt to your particular field of interest.

DECORATIVE PAINTING TECHNIQUES AND DESIGN

Driggers, Susan Goans, *Country Finishes*, Plaid Enterprises, 1988.
Driggers, Susan Goans, *Faux Finishes*, Plaid Enterprises, 1987
Foster, Scottie, *Scottie's Bauernmalerei*, Books 1 to 4*, Scottie's Bavarian Folk Art, 1982, 1983, 1985, 1989.
Innes, Jocasta, *Paint Magic: Home Decorator's Guide to Painted Finishes*, Doubleday, 1985.
Jansen, Jo Sonja, *The Basics of Folk Art I and II*, Jo Sonja's Folk Art Studio, 1981 and 1983.
Jansen, Jo Sonja, *Folk Art Techniques*, Jo Sonja's Folk Art Studio, 1984.
Kneen, Deborah, *The Australian Folk Art Collection*, Tracy Marsh Publications Pty Ltd., Adelaide, 1989.
Koustrup, Birthe, *Wildflower Ideas for China Painting*, Kangaroo Press, 1984.
Folk Art Designs, vol. 1, *Floral Motifs**, (anthology) Pamela Publications, 1985.
* indicates European or North American designs but the principles and techniques involved are universal.

HISTORY

McPhee, John, *Australian Folk and Popular Art in the Australian National Gallery*, Australian National Gallery, Canberra, 1988.

LETTERING

Brown, Phyllis, *Lettering Charts for Students and Artists*, Angus & Robertson, 1988.

WILDFLOWERS

Blombery, Alec M., *What Wildflower Is That?*, Lansdowne Press, 1973.
Buchan, Ursula, & Colborn, Nigel, *The Classic Horticulturist*, Collins /Angus & Robertson, 1988. Includes native and exotic species.
Conabere, E., & Garnet, Ros, J. *Wildflowers of South-Eastern Australia*, Greenhouse, 1987.
Cronin, Leonard, *The Concise Australian Flora*, Reed, 1989. A superb reference book.
Dutton, Ninette, *Wildflower Journeys: With Paintings, Drawings and Diaries by Ninette Dutton*, Macmillan, 1985.
Miller, Constance, *Constance Miller Book of Flowers: Four Seasons of Australian Wildflowers*, Macmillan, 1989.
Weare, Patricia, *Australian Wildflowers*, Collins/Angus & Robertson, 1988.

OTHER SOURCES

You will find Australian calendars, diaries, greeting cards and postcards a useful source of ideas.

INDEX

Note: Page numbers in italics indicate a diagram or illustration.

A

Acacia pycnantha (see golden wattle)
Acacia ulicifolia (see juniper wattle)
acrylic paints 14, 16, 18, 22, 23, 24
acrylic staining 16
Actinotus helianthi (see flannel flower)
Advent Tree, tradition of 95
aerosols 14
Amanita muscaria 32, 51, *51*, 94
Anigozanthos manglesii (see Kangaroo paw)
Aphanopetalum resinosum (see gum vine)
Arts and Crafts Movement 11
asymmetrical designs 37
Australian bindweed 29, *52*, *54*, 70, 79, *105*
Australian hollyhock *52*

B

background techniques 24
balance in design 36
Banksia dentata (see tropical banksia)
Banksia ilicifolia (see holly-leaved banksia)
Baroque style 37
base-coating 16
base-painting 17
Bauernmalerei 11, 36, 51
Beaufortia sparsa (see swamp bottlebrush)
berries *52*
Billy's buttons *31*, *75*, 77
bindweed 29
bisque porcelain 22
black boy 88, *105*
Blandfordia grandiflora (see Christmas bell)
blocking in 17, 24, 34
blue gum 26, *54*, 70, 94, *105*
borders 39, *39*, 40, *40*, *46*, *47*
boronia 46, 54, 70, *101*
Boronia megastigma (see brown boronia)
botanical artist, definition of 53
bottlebrush *41*, 51, *68*, *74*, *89*, 95
bower plant 29, *54*, 70, *79*, *98*, *102*
bower vine 29, *54*, 70, *79*, *98*, *102*
Brachycome iberidifolia (see Swan River Daisy)
brown boronia 54, 70

C

Callistemon macropunctatus (see bottlebrush)
candles 22
    finishing 22
    painting 22
    preparation 22
canvas 20
    finishing 20
    painting 20
    preparation 20
Celmisia longifolia (see snow daisy)
Ceratopetalum gummiferum (see NSW Christmas bush)
Christmas bell *42*, 51, *54*, 70, *91*, 94
Christmas bush *42*, *51*, *62*, 70, 94, 99
Christmas wildflower *32*, *41*, *42*, 51, *51*, *92*, 94, 95
Christmas floral designs *32*, *41*, *42*, 51, *51*, *92*, 94, 95
clematis *44*, 51
Clematis aristata (see native clematis)
Clianthus formosus (see Sturt's desert pea)
clock faces 106
coachwood *44*
colour values 17
common heath (see pink heath)
Convulvulus erubescens (see Australian bindweed)
Cooktown orchid *27*, *56*, 70, *75*, *99*, *105*, *106*
Coolgardie gum (see coral gum)
coral gum 94
coral heath *45*
Correa reflexa (see native fuschia)
crabapple *52*
Craspedia uniflora (see Billy's buttons)
Crinum flaccidum (see Murray lily)

D

daisy 11, *31*, 50
daphne (see native daphne)
Darling lily (see Murray lily)
decorative artist, definition of 53
Dendrobium bigibbum (see Cooktown orchid)
Dendrobium speciosum (see rock orchid)
designs
    asymmetrical 37
    enlarging 34
    negative space in 36, 37
    reducing 34
    repetition 36
    symmetrical 37
    transferring 34, 35
    unity 36
    variety 36
Dryandra formosa 51, *66*, 71

E

embossed lettering 24, 106
enlarging designs 34
Epacris impressa (see pink heath)
Eriostemon myoporoides (see native daphne)
eucalyptus 51
Eucalyptus ficifolia (see red-flowering gum)
Eucalyptus globulus (see blue gum)
Eucalyptus macrocarpa (see mottlecah)
Eucalyptus torquata (see coral gum)
Eucryphia lucida (see leatherwood)
Eustrephus latifolius (see wombat berry)
everlasting daisy *31*

F

fabric 19
  choice 19
  colours 19
  finishing 20
  fixative 20
  heat-setting 20
  paints for 20
  special effects 20
  testing 19
Federation 11
ferns 45, 51, *101*
fernwork, see spatterwork
fibreboard, medium-density 14, 16
filler flowers 35, 38, *38*, 51
filling, wood 15
finishing
  bisque porcelain 22
  candles 22
  canvas 20
  fabric 20
  glass 23
  leather 24
  metal 18
  paper 24
  papier mâché 21
  straw 21
  terracotta 23
  wood 17
flannel flower 11, *31*, 36, *36*, *38*, 50, 52, 56, 70, 74, 76, 89, 90, 91, *101*, *105*
folk artist, definition of, 53
foxglove *52*

G

galvanised metal 18
glass 11, 23
  finishing 23
  painting 23
  preparation 23
  glass paints 23
Glückpilze 51, *51*
golden everlasting *31*, *71*
golden wattle 17, 44, 56, 94
Gossypium sturtianum (see Sturt's desert rose)
Grevillea ilicifolia (see holly grevillea)
grid system 34
guinea flower *30*, 56, 70 *75*, *77*, *105*
gum *12*, *32*, 51, 94, 95, 97
gum vine *43*

H

Hakea laurina (see pincushion hakea)
heath myrtle *45*, 51, *56*, 70, *105*
heat-setting 20
Helichrysum bracteatum (see golden everlasting)
Helichrysum elatum (see white paper daisy)
Helichrysum stirlingii (see Ovens everlasting)
Helipterum roseum (see pink paper daisy)
Hibbertia dentata (see guinea flower)
Hibiscus heterophyllus (see native rosella)
Hinderlooper style 37
hollyhock *52*
holly grevillea *32*, 51, *51*, *58*, 70, *92*, 94, *101*
holly-leaved banksia *42*, 94
Hymenanthera dentata (see tree violet)

I

ironbark *105*

J

juniper wattle *88*, *105*

K

kangaroo apple *30*, *58*, 70, *98*, *105*
kangaroo paw *28*, 70
knots in wood 16

leather 24
  finishing 24
  painting 24
  preparation 24
leatherwood 44, *58*, 70, 97, *105*
lechenaultia 95
Lechenaultia hirsuta (see scarlet lechenaultia)
Leptospermum squarrosum (see peach blossom tea tree)

lettering *88*, 104, 105, 106
lilly pilly *44, 58, 70, 92, 97, 105*
lily of the valley 51, *52*
liner work 16, 17

M

maidenhair fern *45*
Mangles' Kangaroo paw *28, 58, 70*
medium-density fibreboard 14, 16
metal 18
    finishing 18
    painting 18
    preparation 18
Micromyrtus ciliata (see heath myrtle)
Minnie daisy *105*
Minuria leptophylla (see Minnie daisy)
morning glory *52*, 70
Morris, William 11
mottlecah *95*
Murray lily *30, 60*, 70
Myriocephalus stuartii (see poached egg daisy)

N

National Gallery of Australia 12
native clematis *44*, 51, *60*, 70
native daisy *31*, 50, *99*
native daphne *60*, 70
native foxglove *52*
native fuchsia *43, 60*, 70, *94*
native jasmine (see bower plant)
native passion flower *29, 78, 82*
native rosella 50, *60*, 70, *85, 93*
native violet *44, 52, 53, 62*, 70, *77, 79, 100, 105*
negative space, in design 36, 37
non-toxic products 14
NSW Christmas bush *42*, 51, *62*, 70, *94, 99*
numerals *88*, 104, 105, 106

O

oil-based products 14
oil-based varnish 22, 24
oil paints 14, 23
opaque base coat 16
orchid *27, 56, 64*, 70, 71, *99, 106*
Ovens everlasting daisy *31, 62*, 70, *91, 100, 105*

P

Pandorea jasminoides (see bower plant)
paper 24
    finishing 24
    painting 24
    preparation 24

paper daisy *31*
papier mâché 21
    finishing 21
    painting 21
    preparation 21
Passiflora herbertiana (see passion flower)
passion flower *29, 78, 82*
paste wax 17, 18
peach blossom *52*
peach blossom tea-tree *45, 52, 62, 70, 97*
Penetrol 18, 107
permanent marking pen 16, 24, 40
pickling 16
pincushion hakea *42, 62*, 70, *94*
pink boronia *43*
pink heath 25, *64*, 70, *105*
pink paper daisy *31*
Pityrodia teckiana (see native foxglove)
poached egg daisy *31, 64*, 70
polyurethane varnish 17
porcelain 22
primer 18
pressed-type letters 104, 106

Q

Queen Anne's lace 51
Queensland bramble *52, 100, 105*

R

Ranunculus inundatus (see river buttercup)
red-flowering gum *32*, 51, *64*, 71, *95*
reducing designs 34
repetition in design 36
river buttercup *64*, 71, *101*
rock orchid *64*, 71, *105*
rose 11, 50, *50*
rosella 50, *60*, 70, *85, 93*
Rosemaling 36
royal bluebell *27, 66*, 71, *75, 100, 105*
rubbing down 17
rust prevention 18
rust-preventive primer 18
rust remover 18

S

sanding 14, 15, 17, 18
scarlet banksia *32, 77, 98*
scarlet lechenaultia *43, 95*

sealing 16, 21, 22
showy dryandra 66, 71
snow daisy 31
Solanum aviculare (see Kangaroo apple)
spatterwork 12, 12
staining 16
stinkwood 88, 105
straw 21
    finishing 21
    painting 21
    preparation 21
straw flower (see golden everlasting)
stripping, wood 15
Sturt's desert pea 12, 28, 66, 71, 91, 95, 99
Sturt's desert rose 26, 50, 71, 105
surface preparation
    bisque porcelain 22
    candles 22
    canvas 20
    fabric 19
    glass 23
    leather 24
    metal 18
    paper 24
    papier mâché 21
    straw 21
    terracotta 23
    wood 15, 16
swamp bottlebrush 95
Swan River daisy 31, 66, 71, 77, 79
symmetrical design 37

T

tack cloth 15
tannin 16
Tasmanian waratah 95
tea-tree 45, 70, 97
Telopea speciosissima (see waratah)
Telopea truncata (see Tasmanian waratah)
terracotta 23
    finishing 23
    painting 23
    preparation 23
textile medium 19
thickener, use of on fabric 20
toadstool 32, 51, 51, 92, 94
toxicological testing 14
transfer paper 34, 35
transfer pen 19, 35
transferring designs 19, 34, 35
tree violet 45, 51, 52, 68, 71, 105
tropical banksia 41, 68, 71, 105

tulip 11, 52
turpentine 14

U

umbrella fern 105
unity, in design 36
unglazed porcelain 22

V

value of colour 17
variety in design 36
varnish 14, 15
    oil-based 22, 24
    water-based 16, 17, 18, 21, 22, 23, 24
Viola hederacea (see native violet)
violet 52

W

Wahlenbergia gloriosa (see Murray lily)
waratah 11, 11, 25, 36, 50, 50, 51, 53, 68, 71, 74, 75, 84, 89, 95, 96, 97, 99, 100, 105
watercolour paints 24, 106
Waterhousea floribunda (see lilly pilly)
wattle 17, 17, 44, 51, 71, 74, 98
weeping bottlebrush 41, 68, 71, 95
weeping lilly pilly 44
white paper daisy 68, 71
wombat berry 52
wonga vine 70, 98
wood 15
    finishing 17
    painting 16, 17
    preparation 15
    stripping 15

X

Xanthorrhoea australis (see black boy)

Y

yellow hakea 105

Z

zinc coating on metal 18
Zieria arborescens (see stinkwood)